the simplicity project

Win Your Battle with Chaos & Clutter
So You Can Live a Life of Peace & Purpose

By Corie Clark

*This book is dedicated to Ryan, Parker, Morgan, and Brody. I love you all more than you will ever know. You are my why and I would do anything for you. And to all of you who believed in me even when I didn't believe in myself.
I could never have done any of this without God's grace.
So, to Him, I give thanks.*

Copyright © 2014-2022 Corie Clark

All rights reserved. No portion of this book may be reproduced in any manner without written permission except for brief quotations in critical reviews or articles.

All Scripture quotations, unless otherwise indicated, are taken from the Holy Bible, New International Version®, NIV®. Copyright ©1973, 1978, 1984, 2011 by Biblica, Inc.™ Used by permission of Zondervan. All rights reserved worldwide. www.zondervan.comThe "NIV" and "New International Version" are trademarks registered in the United States Patent and Trademark Office by Biblica, Inc.™

ISBN: 978-0-9904995-1-0

Table of Contents

Forward	i
Preface	iii
Introduction	vii
What Is Simplicity To You?	ix
Chapter 1. Stop the Madness	1
Chapter 2. Before We Dive In	5
Chapter 3. It's All About You	9
Chapter 4. Spiritual Health	11
Chapter 5. Physical Health	15
Chapter 6. A Place to Call Home	25
Chapter 7. What Story is Your Home Telling?	28
Chapter 8. The Kitchen	41
Chapter 9. Bathrooms & Bedrooms	53
Chapter 10. Living Spaces	55
Chapter 11. Money, Money, Money	63
Chapter 12. Dream Big	65
Chapter 13. The B Word	68
Chapter 14. Stretch that Green	73
Chapter 15. Bring Home the Bacon	79
Chapter 16. Time is on Your Side	87
Chapter 17. Budget Your Time	92
Chapter 18. Bringing it All Together	101
28 Day Simplicity Project	103
About the Author	135

Forward

What if the words in this book went all the way to the edge? All the way to the top, the bottom, the left, the right? It would drive you crazy, wouldn't it? We need the white space. We need margins.

The same is true with life. We need white space. We need margins.

In The Simplicity Project, Corie confronts this need and supplies a plan for clearing out the chaos and clutter in all areas of your life. Take the 28-Day Challenge and watch your life fill with more peace and more purpose. It's time to reclaim the white space in your life.

Randy Langley

Preface

We all long for a life of more. For living a life of passion and purpose, filled with hope and dreams. A life that makes a difference and changes the world.

But all too often, life just gets in the way. Sounds like a paradox, right? We dream bigger dreams, we struggle, we strive, and we search for meaning and then somewhere along the way, life gets in the way of living. We've got mouths to feed, laundry to do, emails to answer, and deadlines to meet. On top of that, we have clutter filling our homes and our minds and there really seems to be no light at the end of the tunnel. Of course, there are other things that stand in the way of dreaming like fear and the voices in our heads that tell us we're not worthy.

In my case, I was letting the busyness of life keep me from living. The closer I would get to my dream, the farther away I would feel. I pushed through the fear, I faced giants, and I told the voices in my head to sit down and shut up. But I couldn't keep up with the to-do list and being pulled in every direction. So I ended up putting my dreams in the back seat with the voices. This left me in the same position I was in before I remembered what it was like to dream and find purpose. What good is a dream if you're not acting on it? What's the point of having a purpose if you're not living it out?

In the spring of 2008 I found myself sprawled out on my daughter's bedroom floor, crying out to God for more. I didn't know what that *"more"* was. To be honest, I was completely happy with my life. And still am, by the way. But there was something missing and I could not, for the life of me, put my finger on it. All I knew was there was something I needed and it wasn't there. A longing in my soul, in my bones, to do something more with my life.

I had always been an entrepreneur. It's in my blood and as far back as I can remember, I was always dreaming and scheming of a way to make money. I remember being a little girl and wanting to have a parade on my street. I was going to sell tickets to anyone who wanted to watch and would have merch tables where people could buy my handmade gift items, home-grown roses, and fresh squeezed lemonade. If there was a way for me to make something from nothing and turn it into cash, I wanted to try it!

And I think that's what the longing was. I had Jesus, an amazing husband, three beautiful children, and a home to boot. But that tugging was still there and it was starting to get to me.

I dabbled in blogging and failed miserably. I was one of those "coupon bloggers" before I knew it was even a thing. I really just wanted to help people save money and quickly realized there were tons of others doing the same thing making a LOT more money than I was! But, I was making money simply by sharing my expertise, and that was exciting!

It wasn't until 2013 that I really started pursuing my purpose. And since I didn't quite know exactly what that meant or what it was, I decided I'd blog about it. Simply showing up online and sharing my thoughts and experiences to hopefully inspire others to do the same. To live on purpose. My first blog post was about taking that first step. The one we're all scared to take, but once we do, we gain a little more courage.

I had no idea that a simple blog post would lead to a multiple six-figure product based business in less than two years. I'm pretty sure that no entrepreneur or business owner truly comprehends the magnitude of the first step until they're further down the road and can look back at where it all began. Hindsight is always 20/20, right?

In 2014, after about 6 months of blogging, I decided it was time to take the leap and write a book. I was so excited and just knew that this was it. This was my calling and no one would stop me.

Except for myself.

As I tried to pursue my dream of becoming a published author, I quickly realized that my life was in utter chaos. This chaos wasn't something that anyone on the outside looking in could see. But I could see it. I could feel it. I didn't have the time or capacity or energy to focus on my dreams.

If I couldn't win the battle with chaos and clutter, how was I supposed to see my dream come to fruition? How was I supposed to walk out the path of purpose that God put me on? I needed peace so that I could live on purpose. How could I let things like a to-do list and a life of excess take me off the course that I was put here for? It wasn't going to happen. Not on my watch. Maybe a life of more is actually a life of less.

With a list in my hand and a dream in my heart, I decided to go to war. Thus, the Simplicity Project was born.

Introduction

*"Create some margin and watch what God can do.
There are miracles in the margin!"*

I spent 28 days creating margin in our life so that I could live the life I've always dreamed of.

I decided to write a book (*this one you're holding in your hands!*) based on everything I'd learned. I knew there were other people just like me. People trying to live out their purpose but bogged down with the hamster wheel of life. People who longed for more but couldn't keep up with their to-do list, let alone find time to nurture their own souls. So I wanted to share what I had learned with the world.

And that's when everything changed. As people started diving into the book and applying what I shared to their own lives, they started asking for a planner. One that would help them implement everything they had learned. One that would help them create margin in their lives so they could live more purposefully.

This birthed the idea of the Purposeful Planner. I had no idea what the heck I was doing, but I was going for it! And because I had created that margin in our lives, doing exactly what I teach in this book, I had the capacity for a business that would take off right before our eyes.

It's been over seven years since the very first Purposeful Planner hit the market and it has been a wild ride for sure. But I can promise you, if I had not created the margin for it, and kept that margin in place over the last seven years, I would be burnt out and over it.

Work-life balance can be achieved and maintained. But it takes effort. It takes discipline. It takes discernment. And it takes a willingness to live life a little differently.

But isn't that what we're all after? A life that is made up of the desires God puts on our hearts instead of following the cookie-cutter life that everyone else is after?

This revised edition of the Simplicity Project has some minor updates and additions but I felt it was important to keep the bulk of it as is. I may no longer do some of the things I shared, like budgeting to stretch our dollars (now I find more ways to increase our income) or make some of the meals I used to. But, when your life is stretched so incredibly thin, you have to start where you are and take baby steps to get to the life of your dreams.

It's your turn, my friend. Your turn to let go of the chaos and clutter that life so desperately wants you to cling to. Because when you do, you will find the peace and purpose your heart has been longing for.

Are you ready?

To live is the rarest thing in the world. Most people just exist.
 - Oscar Wilde

What Is Simplicity To You?

What comes to mind when you hear the word simplicity? Is it a clean room, crisp white bed sheets, a warm peaceful beach, or maybe a blank canvas? When I think of the word simplicity and picture it in my head, my mind rests. I feel like I can breathe. I picture myself lying in a freshly made bed and just breathing in, breathing out. Soaking in the day and what this life has given me. Sometimes I picture my family sitting in a huge living room that is calm and clean, free of clutter and noise, and just enjoying each other's company. Or laying on a white sand beach with my family and fully enjoying ourselves because everything is as it should be and our responsibilities are only what we've decided they are.

Other times, I picture my grammy back in the 1950's, tending to her family without the gazillion distractions we have today. How simple life was, back then. I'm sure she didn't feel that way, but when I look at pictures of the life my grandparents lived, it was full. Full of life, full of love, full of adventure. They had the time and the energy and the money to do the things they wanted to do with the people they loved.

I can only imagine what it was like to wake up and not have email, voicemail, or schedules to check. To just take care of the household duties, feed the family, and send the kids off to school or to play in the neighborhood. Cooking real food from scratch, picking up a few toys, hanging the laundry to dry in the sun. Living within their means and working diligently to live the life they dreamed. A life full of dreams and purpose.

A simple life, but a full life.

I want that for myself and my family. I want to have the energy, the health, and the freedom to live an active purposeful life. The capacity to run a business that impacts the world without me having to sacrifice precious time with my family. I want less on my to-do list and more time; less complacency and more energy; less burdens and more finance to do what God has called us to do. I want to be able to say, "Yes, we can do that! We can help that family in need." Or, "Yes, we can take that vacation!" Even better, "Yes, we'll do what you've called us to do."

Simplifying my life and ordering my priorities was the key to achieving this life I desired, and the key to you doing so as well.

Take a moment to write down what simplicity looks like to you:

_____
_____
_____
_____
_____
_____
_____
_____
_____
_____

Chapter 1

Stop the Madness

Life does not have to be so complicated. We all know this, yet, we are the ones who complicate it. Every single thing we say yes to or give a go at adds to the complication. Every. Single. One. So we must be intentional with saying, *yes*. and even more intentional with saying, *no*. Whether it's agreeing to take another project or another bite, hitting the snooze button in the morning, buying another shirt we don't need, or staring at the abyss our phones have become, we must begin to identify the impact of each little decision over time. We work and work to buy more stuff. Then, we spend more time taking care of the things we've worked for than we do actually enjoying them.

Ask yourself what the ripple effect will be, even if it may not make a huge difference right now. Is it worth the time and energy?

Sure, another project isn't going to kill me. But it will take away from my time and probably add to my stress, which will in turn cause me to be short with my husband and children and quite possibly cause me to feed them unhealthy fast food because I don't have time to deal with grocery shopping and cooking. Do you see how easy it is for one small project to affect my entire life?

As a family, we've been trying to move at a little slower pace, eat a little healthier, and spend a little less money. We are creating margin in our lives so that we can live on purpose. Saying no a little more to outside activities and instead playing board games together more often; walking to the frozen yogurt store for family dessert. Maybe it's because my kids are growing up too fast; maybe I'm realizing it's completely impossible to keep up with the life we're "supposed to" live. But whatever it is, I like it! And I hope this inspires you to live a life of simplicity as well.

All of the areas we are going to address in this book are connected. Our health, our homes, our finances, and our time all pour into the lives we lead. Unhealthiness leads to unhappiness, which leads to laziness or restlessness. Our schedule becomes affected and we end up spending time on things that actually lead us away from the lives we desire and were created for. You may not always follow this cycle, but this is a reasonable example of how easily being careless in one area of our lives can lead to being unsettled in another area as well and the impact on the greater picture and purpose.

The same goes with self-discipline. If you become disciplined in one area, it's contagious. You begin to feel the sense of accomplishment and let it carry over into other areas.

This is what the Simplicity Project will come down to for you. How much are you willing to invest, change, and sacrifice to live the life of peace that you want? A life that is free to be truly lived on purpose. A life full of meaning and not wasted moments.

I don't offer anything new or profound, and I truly believe that you have what it takes to overcome the chaos. I also know we all learn differently, so what works for me might not work for you. But with a little effort and creativity, you can make this project your own. I'm assuming that if you bought this book, there's something that you want to change; and guess what: nothing will change if you keep doing the same thing. So here's your chance.

Through the Simplicity Project, I share my experiences, failures, and successes to encourage and challenge you. Try new things. Say *no* to others grabbing for your time, even when it's difficult. Get rid of belongings that you don't need or use any more. Just one small step in the right direction will bring you more progress than sitting and hoping and wishing. And that step will lead to the next. This won't happen overnight, so don't be discouraged. Your aim is for a lifestyle change, not a quick fix. I want you to live the life that you've always wanted; free of worry, stress, anxiety, clutter, chaos, and noise. It's how we were created to live, and the Simplicity Project will help guide you there.

> *"When we are completely stretched too thin, we're essentially missing out on being used to the capacity that God intends."*

Stretched Too Thin

It seems as though being stretched too thin is the story of our lives. Whether we're trying to keep up with the Joneses, spending more than we earn, enjoying too many calories, or saying yes too often, we are spent! These days, we hit the ground running. And do I even need to mention the complete information overload that steamrolls us from every angle? There are more websites, blogs, and apps than we can count. And while they are all meant to be helpful, they sure seem to be doing quite the opposite. The more I try to find a new way out, the deeper I find myself in the pit of despair.

I think the only true way to simplify our lives is to start saying no, stop buying things we don't need, and start living a life of intention and purpose.

> *"When a person can't find a deep sense of meaning, they distract themselves with pleasure."*
> *Viktor Frankl*

I think Viktor is spot on. While we've been searching for our purpose and the meaning of life we become so distracted by things that please us. We find pleasure in food, busyness, laziness, shopping, and just about anything we can get our hands on. This creates an endless cycle of temporary pleasure and a continual feeling of emptiness. If we can't stay disciplined and keep our purpose and dreams in the center, we can easily jump ship for the next thing we're attracted to.

I recently heard a sermon on clarity of purpose. It couldn't have come at a more perfect time because this is what I've been doing the past couple of years.; really honing in on what my purpose is and how exactly to live that out.

The pastor talked about creating margin in our lives and being content with what we have. When we create margin in any area, it allows God to move there. When we are completely stretched too thin, we're essentially missing out on being used to the capacity that God intends.

Are you content with using what you already have to fulfill God's purpose in your life? Can you trust him to use you right where you are?

One thing I've learned in the process of living out my purpose is that there is a very real enemy who wants to take me out. If he could just get me to snuggle back into my comfy life, he'd be much happier and leave me alone, until he finds the next way to attack me. I know that if I'm too busy, always distracted, and never content, he's lured me off track. I must remain aware, knowing that he is always lurking, waiting to slip in through my moments of weakness. Allowing for God to work is your path toward peace, and your guardrail from the Enemy.

Chapter 2

Before We Dive In

In this book we will cover four key areas. It is split into those four areas so that you can focus on what is most important to you. You can work on one thing at a time or all of them simultaneously. It is completely up to you. There's even a 28-day challenge at the end of the book for those of you who just need to be told what to do.

Throughout each section, you'll find prompts to work through and places you can take notes or jot down your own ideas and lists. Plus, resources I've used and loved to help me in each of those specific areas. For the digital version of those resources and links to my favorite products and tools to help you even more, go to www.thesimplicityprojectbook.com/resources

I've also included some bonuses for you that can be found in chapter 18.

Simplifying these 4 areas comes down to one thing. Creating margin.

When we create margin, we have room to breathe. Room to allow the more important things to take precedent over the less important.

When we create margin in our health by exercising and eating healthy food, it allows us the freedom to enjoy life because we are rested and have energy. We can even live a little and splurge on a tasty meal, which is perfectly fine! No one wants to live so restricted that there is no freedom.

When we create margin in our homes by getting rid of the clutter, we have room to breathe and enjoy the things that tell our story.

When we create margin in our finances, we have room to give. We are able to help others in need or to take our families on a much needed vacation.

When we create margin in our time, we can say yes to things that align with our dreams and purpose.

I don't want to live my life over capacity because that doesn't allow God to work. I need to give Him some room to do the miraculous. If I am exhausted in every area, I can't do what He wants me to. I know that he enables me to do what I'm supposed to do, but it is my responsibility to make a way for it.

HUGE Disclaimer!

I am not perfect! No, ma'am. Even though I lived and breathed the Simplicity Project and gave my life a complete overhaul, I still have to work at it. There's a reason I needed it and it will be with me forever. There are plenty of days that the laundry piles up, the inbox gets slammed, and we don't keep to our financial plan. But I promise that if you put some of these principles into practice, you will feel peace. You will find more time to live your life on purpose instead of your life living you. My own success with the Simplicity Project is what led me to turn it into a book, so that others can know how to successfully conquer chaos as well.

Also, I completely understand that there are people who are born with a clean house, the dishes done, and the laundry put away. They are out there changing the world and can't find 10 things to put on their to-do list. If that is you, then this book will do you no good except for a laugh or two at the insane amount of work I had to put into living a life of simplicity. I am grateful that you are here on this earth at this time ;)

Section One | Simplifying Your Health

Chapter 3

It's All About You

When we're chasing our dreams and keeping up with our daily lives, often the most neglected person is ourselves. We're so busy making ends meet, taking care of our spouses and children, serving at church, and meeting deadlines, that we forget about the most important person that needs to be tended to.

Several years ago I found myself in a huge rut and just didn't know how to get out of it. Maybe I was depressed; maybe I had a chemical imbalance; or maybe *I* was imbalanced. No matter how hard I tried, I just couldn't climb out. All I wanted to do was stay in bed and not do a thing. I knew I needed help.

I reached out to a friend and she recommended her naturopath. I'm so thankful I opened up and admitted something was wrong. I saw the naturopath for about a year, which cost a small fortune. We discovered some underlying issues that eventually snowballed and resulted in my body not operating the way it was designed to. Getting ample sleep and taking supplements that specifically supported my brain and hormones were exactly what my body needed. It was one hundred percent worth it. My husband wanted his wife back and I'm sure my children wanted their mommy back. Taking some time and investing into my health gave them just that. It was one of the most important decisions we've made; I can't imagine where I might be had I not gotten some help.

Even after getting help and back on the right track, I still have to be careful. It is a constant battle--and I think that's the same for most of us in this day and age. I was feeling so good that I thought I could take on the world...and started letting things slide again. As time went on I found myself slowly traveling down that same path. The harder I worked on my dream and tried to become the person I thought I should, the further my health declined. I was staying up late and getting up early. Not eating right or not eating at all, then binge eating because I was starving. Exercise was at a minimum because somehow I didn't "have the time" and I'm fairly certain that my water intake was far below the recommended amount.

Maybe this sounds familiar to you. Maybe you need some professional or medical help. Maybe you need to talk to a friend. Or maybe you just need to take a step back and assess yourself. Are you getting enough sleep? Are you eating the right food? Are you giving yourself any down time? Do you even feel like your body is operating at its potential? The best thing you can do for your family and friends is make sure you're healthy.

When I am unhealthy, the world around me suffers greatly. Spiritual and physical health work hand in hand. If one is failing, the other will too. I need to be at my optimum health in order to fulfill my purpose here. If I want to live a life of peace and purpose, I'm going to have to get down and dirty. Back to square one. Just me, who I was made to be. All of the Bible studies and self-help books in the world aren't going to give me what time with God and simply taking care of the body he gave me will. So that's where I begin.

Chapter 4

Spiritual Health

When I really started to wake up and realize that I had a purpose from God and needed to fulfill it, I was on fire. I wanted more of Him. I wanted as much as I could possibly fill my brain with. I was giving everything I had to building His kingdom and getting to know Him more. I volunteered in several ministries at church and read every book I could get my hands on. I even started taking a Bible college course. The more I could learn, the better. Or so I thought.

The more I strived to chase my dreams and fulfill God's purpose for my life, the further I felt from Him. How could this be? This was the first time in my life I felt like I was finally getting it, yet I couldn't even feel God in the midst. I was trying to fill a void that could only be filled simply through a relationship with Christ.

As I stripped these things away and focused on him, I could finally hear him speak. I could feel his gentle nudge of *this way, not that. Do this, not that*. And what He was telling me was to just be still. To stop striving and let Him do the work. He was writing me into His story. I didn't need to try to fit Him into mine.

When I remove all of the distractions and just sit in His presence, I feel the peace slowly flow from the top of my head to the bottom of my feet. It really is heaven on earth.

I've always been one to try the next best thing. To read as many books as I can get my hands on and try the latest bible study. None of these things alone are bad, but when they start to replace the relationship between my Father and me, they can be detrimental.

Simplifying your spiritual life will probably be the easiest thing you'll do. Just put away all of the study books for now. There's time for them later. Get your Bible and a journal and just be. Try spending the first fifteen to thirty minutes of your day focusing on Him. Read His word. Ask the Holy Spirit to reveal new things to you. Thank him for all that He's given you. Write these things down. Meditate on them and see what He has to say to you.

Let God's love fill your tank in the morning, not your social media feeds. Allow God to strip away all of the excess so He can reveal what His plans are for you. Let His grace cover all of your failures. They don't matter now; they're just going to be used as stepping stones along the rest of the path.

If you really want to study the word and aren't quite sure where to start, try the SOAP[1] method. It's simple; you don't need a fancy study book, just your bible and a pen and paper. SOAP stands for Scripture, Observation, Application, Prayer. And it's just that simple. Read scripture, write down your observations and how you can apply it to your life. Then pray. When I'm not sure where God's leading me, the SOAP method is what I always fall back on. It's simply Jesus and simply the word. Nothing else.

Another thing I do is journal. I actually keep two journals. Let's get real. I have about twenty on hand, but use two at a time. One is a gratitude journal where I simply write down one line anytime I think of something that I'm thankful for. A kiss from my husband, a hug from my kids, the ocean breeze, my washing machine, anything at all. The other journal is for what I'm learning or what I'm hoping for.

Now, perhaps you're thinking to yourself that you're not a writer. Let me tell you something. You are! You have thoughts and ideas, right? Write them down. Write down what you're thankful for and what you're believing God for. It is so important to write these things down because we often forget if we don't. And then, when God provides for something or leads you into your purpose, you don't even realize it's something you desire. If it's written down, it's proof of where you have been and where you are going and gives Him all the glory.

As you begin to put God first and take time out for yourself every day, you'll begin to feel such an overwhelming inner peace. The worry flees and you find yourself free to be who you were made to be. Living your life on purpose.

Spiritual Health Assessment

On a scale of 1-10, how satisfied are you with your spiritual life?

_____

_____

What is one thing you need to do to start moving towards being completely satisfied in this area?

_____

_____

_____

_____

What are some things you need to let go of in this area?

_____

_____

_____

_____

Chapter 5

Physical Health

Our physical health is just as important as our spiritual health. Isn't it funny how we Americans love to complicate anything and everything? Even when it comes to our health, we complicate it. We have to try the latest fad diet or the trending workout craze, join the fancy gym, or buy expensive equipment.

There are new diets and trends every day. One day grains are good, the next day they're bad. The same goes for red meat. And red wine. The list goes on and on. Our health really doesn't have to be that complicated. We were made to be active and eat healthy food. Food is fuel, so there's no reason to stop eating it; in fact, we must eat to keep these bodies of ours working!

I'm not a doctor or even a nutritionist so I'm not going to give you any medical advice. If that's what you need, please see your doctor. What I can offer you is advice from a wife, mom of three kids, business owner, normal, real-life person who is not blessed with a speedy metabolism that allows me to eat candy bars all day and do five sit-ups before bed to get a flat stomach. It takes work. It takes discipline. It takes trial and error.

Guess what. You don't have to join a fancy gym or hire a nutritionist to get yourself healthy! Say what???! The truth of the matter is, we already have everything we need to live a healthy life. This, too, does not have to be that complicated. Again, we were made to be active and to eat healthy food to keep us strong and able.

We must learn to make our physical selves a priority. Pay attention to how you are feeling and what your body is telling you. If something doesn't seem right, it probably isn't.

Food

First things first. What you put in is what you get out. If you're feeding yourself junk, you're going to feel like junk. Food is not the devil. Your body was created to eat good food! Good food equals good fuel. Bad food equals bad fuel. No food equals no fuel. Get it?

If there's anything I've learned about food, it's that if God made it, it's probably good for me. The amount of processed food we feed our families these days is insane. And it's not doing anybody any good. We all know from grocery store price tags that fresher equals more expensive. This is not an excuse to eat poorly; it just means that we need to be smart with our purchases. That's why I try to buy what's in season; it's fresher and less expensive.

If you start feeding yourself food that God has made and not all that processed crap, you're taking a huge step in the right direction. Drink tons of water. Eat food that God made. Avoid processed foods. See, you already know this. Nothing new here. This probably goes without saying, but I'm going to say it anyway: stop eating crap! I know; it's so hard! Believe me, I know. I love candy. Way too much. It's my splurge--once in a while. There's just something about Cadbury Eggs, Lemon Heads, and Hot Tamales that I can't refuse! But I don't let junk food take over my diet, and you shouldn't either.

My family has been on a journey to wellness for several years now. It's definitely a process but the more you work at it, the easier it gets. We've eliminated almost all processed foods. I say almost because we're not perfect. I'll buy granola bars for the kids once in a while and we love ourselves some chips & queso quite often. And who doesn't love a hot greasy pizza? But for the most part, we eat clean. We avoid processed sugar and foods as much as possible. We avoid soda and juices because they're loaded with sugar and other nasty ingredients. You get the picture, now try it for yourself!

Exercise

I've never been one for fancy gym memberships. I just think they're overpriced and inconvenient. We did have a family membership several years ago when the kids were younger. It was a good price and allowed me to work out while the kids played. But even at a good price it eventually became more of a burden than a tool to help our family.

On top of the monetary cost, there is a large time cost that is often forgotten when signing up for that must-have membership. How much time will it take you to drive back and forth? Walking in from the car, checking in, dropping your belongings in the locker room, running in to so and so. Now your 45-minute workout has turned into ninety minutes.

This was a constant battle for me. On days that I wanted to get a workout in but knew I didn't quite have the time, I'd just not go at all. Other times I would go for it and then be discouraged by the block of time it took from my day.

What good is gaining our health if I'm stretching our money and trying to squeeze the gym into my schedule? I may have been relieving one stress but I was adding two more!

To stay in shape, I go on walks with my husband and/or kids quite often. To get my strength in, I've bought some weights, kettlebells, and resistance bands. Since I'm not good at making up my own routine I use videos. I love having Amazon Prime because there are tons of free streaming workout videos and there are quite literally thousands of apps and videos on YouTube as well! Free content is everywhere.

This does not mean that I'll never get a gym membership again, I just think that getting in a workout doesn't have to be that complicated. If your attempt at getting healthy is affecting other areas of your life in a negative way, maybe it's time to simplify.

Make yourself a priority. Set aside time to get your heart pumping and your muscles working. If the weather is decent, like it always is here in Southern California, then a simple walk or jog outside should suffice. Don't just rely on cardio. Cardio is good for your heart and your body, which was created to move. But it's strength work that will build lean muscle and burn fat. Add in some weights, kettlebells or resistance bands a couple of days a week and you're golden.

I am no longer in sunny So Cal and am learning to walk in the rain, freezing weather, and insane humidity here in Middle Tennessee. Not fun at all but still a big priority! It's my alone time to worship, pray, or listen to a podcast!

The amount of information regarding exercise out there is staggering. You can find workouts of any kind on the internet. It's just a matter of discipline. Be selfish with your time and get the workout in. Your body will thank you. Especially when you have energy to play with your kids, start fitting comfortably in your clothes and feeling more confident in your skin.

If you have the time and the money to get a gym membership, then by all means, get one. They're useful and help keep you accountable, especially if you workout with a friend, a spouse, or attend a class. But seriously. If it's going to put a strain on your budget or your schedule, do something else!

Sleep

For a long period of time I was overworking myself. I was completely sleep-deprived, trying to get everything done I needed to, while more responsibilities continued to pile up. I foolishly believed that I needed to tackle the to-do list, write my book, be a good wife, homeschool my kids, and do any and every single thing that crossed my mind if I wanted to get anywhere in life.

I've found that getting up early is the answer to getting more things accomplished; but, only when going to bed earlier! When I was first working on my dream, I was waking at 5 am. I loved being up 2 hours before my kids. I had time to read my Bible, journal, write, work out, and start breakfast. All the while, I was still going to bed between 11 and 12 at night. After several months of burning the candle at both ends, I was starting to suffer. I was irritable and short-tempered; I couldn't focus on a single thing; and I started gaining weight.

Here's what I found. Get up early. It's great. It's wonderful, in fact. But go to bed early too. I know that sleep requirements are different for everyone. Men, for the most part, do better with less sleep than women and some of us just might need more than others. Personally, I need seven to eight hours of sleep at night. I started going to bed at the same time and waking up at the same time. I noticed that after a while, it became routine and my body's internal clock set itself. Just stay consistent.

Again, what works for my family might not work for yours. My kids are getting older and stay up a little later. This means I go to bed later because I want time alone with my husband at night. If I wanted to keep getting up at 5 a.m., I would have to go to bed at the same time as my kids. So I've adjusted my schedule and stay up until about 11, then get up around 6. Sure, I only have one hour alone in the morning but it's worth it to have more time with my husband. Figure out what works for you and your family and then stick to it. You will be so thankful to get on a consistent sleep schedule, and you'll flourish in other areas of your life because of it.

With all this being said, my health is not perfect. It's a journey and it will last until the day I die. In fact. At this moment I could probably drop fifteen to twenty pounds! The only way to win is with discipline. So let's cheer each other on and lift each other up on this path to good health.

Physical Health Assessment

On a scale of 1-10, how satisfied are you with your overall physical health?

_____

_____

What are some things you need to do to start moving towards being completely satisfied in this area?

_____

_____

_____

_____

What are some things you need to let go of in this area?

_____

_____

_____

_____

On a scale of 1-10, how satisfied are you with the food you're fueling your body with?

_____

_____

What are some things you need to do to start moving towards being completely satisfied in this area?

_____

_____

_____

_____

What are some things you need to let go of in this area?

_____

_____

_____

_____

On a scale of 1-10, how satisfied are you with your sleep?

_____

_____

What are some things you need to do to start moving towards being completely satisfied in this area?

_____

_____

_____

_____

What are some things you need to let go of in this area?

_____

_____

_____

_____

Health Highlights

Spend time in God's word.
Journal.
Pay attention to how you feel.
Get plenty of sleep.
Drink plenty of water.
Food equals fuel.
Avoid processed foods.
Move your body.

My favorite health resources can all be found at corieclark.com/simplicityresources

Section Two | Simplifying Your Home

Chapter 6

A Place to Call Home

Home is where it all begins.
Where you get to decide what you love most and can't live without.
Let your home tell your story...
Nate Berkus

Home is not made of walls and a roof; it is made by who and what is inside of it. My husband and I learned that lesson the hard way when we lost the first house we had ever purchased in 2008. We were living the American dream and doing what everyone told us to do. We were completely clueless and were told to do anything in our power to keep the house. So, we did what any other couple in their late twenties and early thirties would do. We dumped every cent we had into trying to save the house. When we were just about out of money we decided not to fight for it anymore and handed the keys over.

The six months of trying to save the house were treacherous. I did tons of praying, hoping, wishing, and learning. Of course, I learned a thing or two about buying homes, but the most important thing I learned is that it doesn't matter who owns the home we live in or where it is even located for that matter. What matters is my family and that I make them feel at home no matter what.

In our 25 years of marriage my husband and I have moved eleven times! Yuck! I hate that we have moved so much. But, it's just the way life has taken us and it does have its benefits. It definitely makes us reassess all of our belongings and forces us to purge every once in a while because we just don't want to move things that are not important.

Sometimes I just wish we could own a home that is big and lovely and has a huge backyard with chickens and cows. I want to host dinner parties and have guests stay in their own room. But I'm thankful for what I have and want it to represent our family as best as it can.

At the time of writing the original version of this book, we were living in Southern California and had made a move that was strictly for location. We wanted to be closer to church, friends, and the beach. It was by far the biggest change we've made.

Living in Orange County meant that we had to sacrifice square footage. Like, major square footage! We crammed five people, two cats, and a dog into a 1,200 square foot condo. Tell me about it. We had all three kids in one room. They were such troopers and I am so thankful that they really neer seem to be bothered by it. There were plenty of days that I felt like the walls were closing in and I just wanted to run away! But, in all honesty, we really did love living there. Being close to friends and to the ocean was far more important to us than having a huge home.

No matter how hard we tried or how much we got rid of, we just couldn't seem to get a handle on the mess and the clutter. The more I would focus on just being a good wife and mom and trying to fulfill my purpose, the more out of control the house seemed to become. I hated the fact that picking up and cleaning was taking up so much of my time. Time that I could spend playing with my kids, helping someone in need, blogging, or writing my book.

Some of these things are just inevitable and have to be addressed almost daily, especially in the early stages of parenting. Oh, how I remember the days of picking up toys four hundred and thirty-seven times, cleaning up spilled Cheerios, and the endless loads of laundry. I promise you, young mamas out there, this does get easier. For now, just breathe, pick up, and repeat.

Even though my kids are older now, it seemed the house was always falling apart. I had to find a way to get things under control. I couldn't let things like chores keep me from living out my purpose. I wanted my home to tell my story.

Maybe you feel the same way. Maybe It's time to let your home tell your story.

Chapter 7

What Story is Your Home Telling?

What does your home say about you? Maybe an even better question to ask is what do you want your home to say?

I remember growing up and visiting others' homes. The ones that stand out are the ones that I was the most uncomfortable in. There's nothing worse than walking into a home and not feeling welcome. Feeling like you can't touch anything or just sit back and relax. Or even worse, not knowing where you can stand or sit because it's such a disaster. I can't tell you how many times I've felt bad for my company because my house was less than presentable.

Then there were the homes that I felt at home, the ones where I could be myself in. I could relax and enjoy the people I was visiting because I wasn't worried about what I was touching or where I should sit.

It's time to make an assessment of your home. Room by room, closet by closet; just really get a good look at everything. Walk through each room and write down how you want it to look and what you want it to feel like. Write it as if it's already done.

Here's what I wrote for my home assessment:

I live in a home that is welcoming and inviting. Where people can come in, kick their shoes off and sit and talk for hours. Where kids can run through the house and not worry about breaking things. Where people live and learn and grow. Where people are comforted, fed, and loved.

When I walk in the front door, a fresh, crisp, and inviting scent welcomes me. The entry hall is free of laundry and clutter; only the keys are hanging on the key hook. The entry table is free of clutter; displaying our favorite pictures and candles.

The kitchen counter is clean and clear of any unnecessary items. The kitchen table is clean and displays a fresh bouquet of flowers and yummy food for family and friends to devour.

All of the kids' school items are put away in their rightful place. Papers are filed. Books are on the shelves.

The living room is clean and free of toys and remote controls. Only a tray on the coffee table and a basket for my daily reading is on the side table.

The staircase has no "put away" items to trip on. Upstairs, each bedroom is clean and dressers are free of clutter. The bathrooms are clean; counters are cleared.

Our home is ready for my family and any guest and welcomes all with love and acceptance.

Did that sound like Martha Stewart or what? But really, that is how I want our home to feel. Not obsessive. Not sterile. Not perfect. Just peaceful.

Use this space below to write what you want your home to say about you.

_____

_____

_____

_____

Assessment

Looking at what we are starting with and knowing what we want to finish with can completely overwhelm us. When I am overwhelmed, I simply don't want to do anything. Let's get real. I'd rather lie in bed and eat bon bons all day and see what all my friends are up to on Instagram.

The best way that I've found to tackle a problem is to face it, head on. Verbalizing or writing down what needs to be done makes it actually seem more attainable.

When I assessed my home, I started with a good old-fashioned list. I walked through the entire house and wrote down the actual tasks that needed to be done to achieve that feeling.

This became my master list. I'll show you what mine looked like and then I want you to make yours. Don't worry; you don't have to tackle this all at once. You just need to get it written down so that you can see that it is in fact attainable and to keep track of your progress.

Here's what my list looked like:

Entry
Put away shoes and extra items hanging on key hook.
Put laundry in its place.
Clear and dust the entry table.

Kitchen
Purge items that we no longer use or love.
Only leave out small appliances that are completely necessary for everyday use.
Clean sink and counter.

Dining Room {this also serves as our homeschool room so it is ALWAYS a disaster}
Purge school items we no longer use.

File papers that need to be filed.
Find homes for smaller items like pens, books, etc.

Living Room
Purge magazines.
Find a home for all of the remotes.
Put games away.
Only put daily reading out; everything else belongs on the bookshelf.

Staircase
Put away all of the things that are waiting there for me.

Master Bedroom
Organize desk.
Clear dresser of laundry.
Mend the clothes in the mending pile.
File papers.
Hang pictures.

Kid's Room
Purge old toys.
Put toys and books where they belong.
Clear the top of the bookshelf.

Bathrooms
Clear counters.
Purge items under skink.
Clean.

Garage
Purge items we don't love or use.
Organize cabinets.

Once I had that list, I felt like I'd won half the battle. Seeing it written gave me so much freedom because I realized it wasn't as bad as I thought. It's like the whole "How do you eat an elephant?" scenario. One task at a time, I could achieve the peaceful home I had been longing for. Some of the tasks can be done in a few minutes while others might take a whole day. But knowing is seriously half the battle in this case.

Now it's your turn. Grab a pen and use the space below or print out your master list found in the free bonuses in chapter 18. Go through each area of the house and write down anything and everything that needs to be done to achieve what you want your home to look like.

Entry

_____
_____
_____

Kitchen

_____
_____
_____

Dining Room

_____
_____
_____

Living Room

_____
_____
_____

Master Bedroom

_____
_____
_____

Master Bathroom

_____
_____
_____

Bedroom Two

_____
_____
_____

Bedroom Three

_____
_____
_____

Bathroom Two

_____
_____
_____

Garage

_____
_____
_____

Office

_____
_____
_____

Other

_____
_____
_____

No Regrets

Before we dive into getting rid of anything and everything in sight, let's address something. Not all clutter is bad. Some of it just needs a different place to sit in your home. Or maybe it needs to be stored for a season.

I was part of an online community a while back that highly encouraged you to get rid of anything and everything. And I mean *everything*.

I completely understand the point. And maybe they just weren't sentimental in any way shape or form. But, I don't think you need to make any rash decisions about things you might wish you had down the road. And I'm not talking about an old pair of socks or a completely burnt out candle. I'm talking about things that were possibly given to you by a loved one that has passed or something from your childhood that leads you down memory lane. I know full well that keeping a trinket that I got from my grammy is not going to bring her back or replace her, but I do like holding something that I know was once in her hand, and I know was a gift from her.

After my grammy passed away it was such a blessing to go through my grandparents' old belongings. I was so thankful that my grandparents kept things like old newspapers, Bibles, journals, records from the business that they owned, and photographs, just to name a few. At this moment, a current newspaper may seem insignificant to us. But in 50 years, maybe your grandson will think it's really special to get a glimpse of what it was like to live in the good 'ole days.

I say all of this so you can just be mindful of the things you throw out. This doesn't mean you keep every single thing. I don't want you to end up being a hoarder, claiming, *"Corie told me to keep everything that had sentiment."* Just be sure to not regret tossing something. When you've decided what items you're going to hang on to, find a special home for them so they don't end up lost or thrown out. A hope chest or a certain drawer or even a plastic container will suffice.

Clear That Clutter

We spend more time taking care of the things we've worked for than we do actually enjoying them. It's time to make some hard decisions on what really matters and what's worth spending time on. Everything you own needs to be tended to. Either washed, dusted, cleaned, or repaired. It all requires work. When we started asking ourselves this question it made it very simple to start getting rid of stuff that wasn't worth our time and energy.

I used my master task list, set my timer for fifteen minutes and started chipping away. I would get as much done in those fifteen minutes as possible. If I worked too long on a specific project, I would get discouraged and frustrated and want to give up. Of course there were times that I worked longer because the kids were gone or I had help from my husband. But, I made amazing progress just spending 15 minutes a day checking things off the list.

I used this same process, outlined below, in each area of our home. It seemed to work well because there's no sense in organizing and cleaning something that you're going to get rid of, Right?

1. Clear all visible spaces of clutter.
2. Go through cabinets and shelves.
3. Organize.
4. Clean.

When we really started purging the things that we didn't need or love anymore, we had to figure out what to do with them. Not everything was trash. Most of the items we wanted to get rid of were in excellent condition and some had a decent resale value.

Since we lived in a condo complex, garage sales just really weren't an option. There was a community garage sale a couple of times a year, but since those sales usually don't attract a big turnout, we found it wasn't worth our participation. Thus, Craigslist, Amazon, and eBay became our best friends. Not to mention the addition of Facebook Marketplace and many other apps since the first writing of this book!

Any items that weren't worth our time of listing were immediately donated. Everything else got listed so that we could make a little extra money. Now, even my kids have fallen in love with eBay. Anytime they want to upgrade their electronics or just aren't using what they have any more, they have me list them on eBay. They've earned quite a bit of money on old handheld games and devices, and even nice toys that were still in excellent condition.

Everyone's situation is different, so you really need to just think about what will work best for you. If you don't have a lot of extra time on your hands to list items or have a garage sale and don't need the extra money then maybe you should just donate them. If something is undesirable because of damage or wear and tear, toss it.

Here is a brief explanation of how we decide what we will do with each particular item.

Use this guide to decide what you will do with it.

Donations:
- Clothing, unless it is designer and in excellent condition
- Old toys with no resale value
- Children's books
- Toiletries
- Small trinkets / vases
- Dishes, unless it's a complete set
- Kitchen gadgets
- Sheets
- Towels
- Picture frames

eBay / Facebook Marketplace / Apps
- Designer clothing / shoes
- Small electronics {iPods, etc.}
- Video Games

- Dishes {complete sets}
- China
- Crystal
- Small kitchen appliances
- Jewelry
- Watches
- Book sets
- Toy sets

Craigslist:
- Furniture
- Small kitchen appliances
- Computers
- Bikes
- Toys
- Camping gear

Amazon:
- Books
- DVDs
- CDs

Listing your items online is very painless. It just takes a bit of time. I absolutely love the apps that make listing items take much less time. And my favorite thing about Amazon is I can send all of my books to them in one shipment and they'll take care of shipping them as they sell them for me. If your budget is tight and you could use the extra money, I highly suggest selling the items that have a decent value.

Cleaning

I'm not going to tell you how to clean. We all hate it, but it has to be done. Here are my suggestions for keeping it simple.

- You don't need 137 cleaning supplies. Most of your cleaning can be done with water, vinegar, and baking soda.
- Keep one complete set of your most used cleaning supplies and rags under each cabinet so you're not running all over the house looking for something.
- Wipe down your surfaces quickly and run the brush around the toilet every day. It takes thirty seconds and will save you from deep cleaning for longer periods of time.
- Do one load of laundry every day. This will keep the endless loads from creeping up on you.

Cleaning supplies that I keep on hand.
- Laundry Detergent
- Bleach
- Dishwashing Detergent
- Dish Soap
- Multi-purpose Cleaner
- Baking Soda
- Vinegar

One thing I don't take the time to do is make my laundry soap. I would love to. I really would. And, someday, maybe I will. But for now, that would just complicate things and I'm trying to simplify. I do make my own multi-purpose cleaner though. And honestly it's fast, cheap, and cleans really well. I also use a baking soda mixture when I need to scour something.

Multi Purpose Cleaner With Vinegar
Use a 24 oz. spray bottle and pour in 1 cup of white vinegar. Fill the rest of the bottle with water and shake well. For disinfecting you can use more vinegar. You can also add a few drops of essential oils if you prefer!

Baking Soda Scrub

In a small bowl put 1/4 cup of baking soda. Slowly mix in water until you have a paste.

Use this to scour sinks, tubs, etc.

We use small rags for all of our cleaning. They can be tossed in the laundry after each use so they don't harbor the germs that sponges do. We also avoid using paper towels as much as possible to save on cost and clutter.

Chapter 8

The Kitchen

When things are feeling out of control in our home, I always go back to the kitchen. A clean and organized kitchen always makes me feel like the rest of the house is pretty clean too. I don't know why; it just does.

The kitchen is the main hub in just about every home. It's where people gather. No matter the age or stage of life, everyone loves food and food is in the kitchen. For us, even though our kitchen is extremely tiny, it's still where everyone gravitates to.

Nothing makes me feel like my kitchen is caving in on me more than a cluttered counter and having to run from one side to the other trying to get different items that I need for a meal. I couldn't kick my family out of the kitchen, so I needed to create a space that, although small in size, felt open and inviting.

I started by clearing my counters. I made sure that my counters only held the items that we used every day. Anything else had to find a new home in a drawer or cabinet. The only thing that stays out that isn't used daily is my Kitchen-Aid stand mixer because that thing weighs as much as I do and I'm not going to try and drag it out of a cabinet every time I need it. Just clearing some space on the counters helped me feel like I had more room and less clutter. The less I have to look at, the more free my mind feels.

Next I found anything and everything I didn't need or use any more. Out it went! This included the pantry and fridge too. I dumped everything that was expired or was just flat out junk that we shouldn't even have anyway. Remember, you don't need to eat it just because you bought it. Better in the trash than on your hips, right?

I dream of the day that I have a perfectly organized pantry like the ones you see on Pinterest. But, until then, I will do my best and use what I have. I love mason jars and they are perfect for organizing your pantry. I keep a variety of sizes on hand and use them for everything. From spices and baking ingredients to beans and cereal. You name it, it goes in a mason jar. I can't tell you how many times I've gone to clean out the pantry and found bags and boxes that were practically empty and just taking up space. Keeping things in mason jars shows you exactly what you have and how much of it is left.

Rearranging is also helpful. Keep dishes stored above the dishwasher for easy unloading; spices and oils next to the stove for easy cooking; food near your biggest prep area for ease in cooking. Being organized and prepared will save you countless headaches and tons of time.

Menu Planning

I cannot emphasize enough the importance of having a menu plan and a well-stocked pantry and fridge. This will save you hundreds of dollars, hours upon hours of your precious time, and will help you to stay healthy because you're not eating out all of the time.

I really do not like cooking. Like, at all. My husband actually does a lot of the cooking around here when he is home. But when he works up until dinner time, it's my responsibility to have a meal prepared, or some sort of plan at least. Sadly, I fail miserably at this and often have no plan whatsoever. This always ends in a last minute, bad decision, of take-out or drive thru.

Gross!

I came up with a system years ago for our family and I hope it will work for yours too. Remember, this is just a plan. It's not set in stone.

It's not a rule. Take it and adapt it to your family's lifestyle. And just because I came up with it years ago doesn't mean I always stick to it. {I just admitted my weakness for drive-thrus to you!} But I promise you, when I do, it saves us so much time and money.

First, I will make a list of twenty of our go-to meals. I ask the kids and my husband for their input too, because I really want to know what meals they enjoy and aren't just kindly gagging down just so they can survive. Then I make a list of the main ingredients that are in all of those in order to make my well-stocked pantry and fridge list. Of course, produce can't be stored for too long, so I do have to make additional grocery trips during the week. But, the meat can be frozen and the canned foods and seasonings can be stored for quite some time, making meal planning much easier.

For the meal to make it onto my list of 20, it has to meet these criteria:

1. Healthy {For the most part}
2. Easy to make
3. Affordable

Having this list is a tremendous help when I'm making my menu plan and grocery list each week. If everything goes according to plan, all I should have to get at the grocery store is perishables and anything that needs to be restocked. Notice I said if. Believe me; I still fail at this. But, having a plan and a master list is incredibly helpful.

When I sit down to make my menu for each week, I need to know what the week is going to look like in terms of what the family's schedule is. I'll usually try to spread a couple of the meals out for the busy days. On Sundays we usually have leftovers because we get home later from church. Mondays and Thursdays are the only days right now that we don't have any set activities, so I know that I can spend more time preparing and cooking on those days. I also know that on Wednesday nights we don't have time to cook. We actually have to eat in the car between sports and church. The best thing I can do is make something on Monday or Tuesday that leaves enough leftovers for us to have dinner on Wednesday. If I don't, we'll certainly be hitting the drive-thru. We usually eat out on Friday night. It's the end of the week and we're all pretty drained. After homeschooling, working, ballet, church, and everything else, we all just need a break! On Saturdays we have time for preparation and also often end up going to friends' houses or having company over.

Here's what an average week looks like in our home:

Sunday - Leftovers

Monday - Regular meal

Tuesday - Slow cooker or pressure cooker meal

Wednesday - Leftovers

Thursday - Regular meal

Friday - Eat out

Saturday - Regular meal

This plan is always evolving depending on what season we're in, if school is in session, if there are holidays and birthdays, or if we just want to change things up. I have learned to not get so worked up when things don't go according to plan and to always have some extra food when I can't stick to the original menu.

When I'm feeling really organized, I use the small sticky notes and write each of the twenty meals on them. I then place them on different days throughout the month. This allows me to move things around when plans change or when I decide something might work better in its place. This is extremely helpful in planning my grocery shopping and cooking because I have an idea of what's coming up in the next week.

Try planning your menu for at least a week and see just how much time and energy it will save you.

A Well Stocked Pantry & Fridge

There's really nothing worse than preparing a meal and realizing you need to run to the store for one more thing. My poor husband has had to stop at the store on his way home from work more times than I'd like to admit. Having a well-stocked pantry, fridge, and freezer are just as important as making your menu plan. Once I've established our master meal list, I then use that to create a master pantry and fridge list. Just by looking over the list at each meal I pretty much know what all I need. Then I'll scan the recipes to make a list of the seasonings I need to keep on hand. My family loves Mexican food so I tend to keep a lot of Mexican spices in stock, and even make my own taco seasoning. Just knowing what your family eats the most will help you determine how much of each item you need to keep handy.

Pantry

Having a pantry that is well stocked and organized will work wonders with your menu planning. I prefer to use mason jars of various sizes because they're glass, which means no chemicals, they stack nicely, and I can see what's inside right when I open the cabinet. I even use them to put cereal, crackers, and similar items in once the boxes have been opened.

I use the small mason jars to store my seasonings in. They're the perfect size to dump an average seasoning bottle into, so any seasonings you use more often can be bought in bulk and poured in. Having all of my seasonings in the same size jars might be an OCD thing but I just like having everything look the same and see what's in the jars without having to look at labels. I just use a sharpie to write what the seasoning is on the lid. Or, if you're really crafty, you can make some cute labels.

I use the large mason jars to put dry items in like popcorn, beans, pasta, rice, etc. This has helped in keeping the pantry tidy and, like I said with the spices, lets you see what you have. How many times have you forgotten that little bag of popcorn or rice because it's laying flat and hiding behind something taller?

Fridge

We currently have a very small refrigerator so I'm not able to keep it as well-stocked as I would like. I can't stock it with more than two or three weeks of food. I load that baby up as much as I can, but I sure would love to have an extra freezer nearby!

We try to keep our leftovers front and center so they aren't forgotten. As soon as they slip behind something else, we have a new science experiment brewing! I scan the fridge as often as possible to get rid of those lovely little containers as well as anything that we just aren't going to use.

Batch Freezer Cooking

I have yet to be consistent with bulk freezer cooking. I've done it on several occasions and I absolutely love having meals stocked up in the freezer and ready to cook. I just can't commit to giving up an entire day and several weeks of our grocery budget to do it all of the time. Instead, I do smaller batches of freezer cooking.

This means that when I am cooking, I cook at least double the amount of food and freeze half of it for a future meal. I figure if I'm going to be cooking it anyways, I might as well cook more to save time in the future. Usually, it doesn't even add to my cooking time. For instance, I'll cook about 5 pounds of ground turkey at once and season it with my taco seasoning mix. I'll put half of it in a freezer bag and the other half is for dinner. It's still more than enough for that meal, and usually leaves meat for lunch the next day or two.

Here is a list of the things that I always cook extra of and freeze 1/2 for later.

- Taco meat
- Ground turkey {plain}
- Ground sausage
- Lasagna
- Pancakes/waffles {reheat in your toaster}
- Breakfast sausage
- Bacon
- Chili
- Soup
- Cookie Dough

One more thing that I started doing, and it's worked out wonderfully, is preparing smoothie bags in advance. I use the quart size freezer bags and fill them with enough ingredients to make two smoothies. The nice thing is you can load them with spinach and kale and not have to worry about it going bad. I'll make as many as I can with the ingredients I have on hand, label them, and pop them in the freezer. Then the kids can grab a bag, throw the contents in the freezer, add some water, and blend. Easy peasy!

If you have the time and energy, bulk freezer cooking is a terrific way to save time and money. You can have a month's worth of meals stocked in your freezer, and it will only take you one day to prep them. Consider joining forces with several friends to split up the work and the cost. Pop open a bottle of wine and it's a party!

Maybe smoothies and freezer cooking aren't your thing. And that's okay! The reason I share what I do is to give you ideas on how you can save time and effort for your family. Think of the things you love to eat on a regular basis. Then, ask yourself how you can make that process easier!

If you're not sure where to even start, here is my Master Meal List and Pantry & Fridge / Freezer list. You will notice that I do not have a master list for breakfast and lunch. We keep breakfast simple with eggs. Once in a while I'll splurge on cereal or make the kids pancakes or waffles. Lunch is mostly salads or left overs. But, I do add our mostly used breakfast and lunch items to the Pantry & Fridge list. I also only have the produce that we use all of the time. Any other that I buy is decided once I make our weekly menu.

Master Meal List { Top 20 }

1. Chili
2. Taco Soup
3. Spaghetti Squash and Sausage
4. Chicken Potato Casserole
5. Tacos
6. Lasagna
7. Enchiladas
8. Breakfast For Dinner
9. Meatball Pizza
10. Barbecued Chicken and Brussels
11. Baked Potato Bar
12. Tostadas
13. Taco Salad
14. Slow Cooker Chicken
15. Burrito Bowls
16. Pulled Pork
17. BBQ Shredded Chicken
18. Pasta and Sausage or Meatballs
19. Carnitas
20. Chicken Stir Fry

Your Top 20 Meal List

(also available in your bonuses and The Purposeful Planner)

1. _____
2. _____
3. _____
4. _____
5. _____
6. _____
7. _____
8. _____
9. _____
10. _____
11. _____
12. _____
13. _____
14. _____
15. _____
16. _____
17. _____
18. _____
19. _____
20. _____

Well Stocked Pantry List

Fridge / Freezer
Ground Turkey 5-10 lbs.
Chicken Breasts 5-10 lbs.
Italian Sausage 5 lbs.
Breakfast Sausage
Bacon 5lbs.
Pork Shoulder 5lb.
Frozen Fruit
Cheddar Cheese 2-4 lbs.
Eggs 5 doz.
Milk
Half & Half
Greek Yogurt
Crushed Garlic
Lettuce
Carrots
Peppers

Pantry
Canned
Black Beans
Kidney Beans
Pinto Beans
Canned Tomatoes
Crushed Tomatoes
Tomato Sauce
Tomato Paste
Chicken Broth

Condiments
Ketchup
Mustard
Mayo
Barbecue Sauce
Olive Oil
Coconut Oil
Avocado Oil
Vinegar
Red Wine Vinegar
Balsamic Vinegar

Dry
Coffee
Tortillas
Pasta
Spaghetti Squash
Potatoes
Onions
Garlic
Bread

Baking/Seasonings
Flour
Sugar
Brown Sugar
Baking Soda
Baking Powder
Corn Starch
Vanilla
Chocolate Chips

Salt
Pepper
Chili Powder
Chili Peppers
Cumin
Paprika
Thyme
Basil
Oregano
Rosemary
Parsley
Nutmeg
Allspice
Cloves

Chapter 9

Bathrooms & Bedrooms

Bathrooms

The bathroom is the second place I hit when we need to give our home a good declutter and cleaning session, probably because it's small and can be taken care of quickly. This is done in the same fashion as the kitchen. I clear the counters and toss all the junk. Old makeup, samples of shampoo I'll never try, broken combs…You know the drill. Toss, toss, toss!

Then, I dig into the drawers and under the sink. I don't know why, but my bathroom drawers love to collect so much crap. Bobby pins, combs, clips, nail clippers, all of the little things that you can never find when you actually need them.

I put some small organizers {you could use mason jars too} in the drawers to hold the smaller items. I also invested in an acrylic makeup caddy. I use a lot of makeup. Not all at once. But, I do like to have a variety. The caddy keeps my collection organized and I can just keep it under the sink when I'm not using it.

Speaking of under the sink. Ugh! I hate having to dig around, so I added a wire shelf that is high enough to put a shoe box size container beneath it. This gives me more storage space, and I do a lot less digging around looking for things.

As you're clearing the clutter in the bathroom, be sure to get rid of anything and everything that you're never going to use. There always seems to be half used bottles of lotions and potions that promise to make you look younger and firmer. If you didn't love them, there's no sense in keeping them.

Bedrooms

Our bedrooms should be a place where we find rest and solitude. They should be a place of peace, not chaos. All too often our bedroom ends up being the dumping ground for loose stuff. Piles of laundry that need to be put away, papers that need to be filed, and pocket change move in and make themselves comfortable.

I tackled the bedrooms in the same way I did the kitchen and bathrooms. I cleared the clutter from the dresser, end tables, and desk. Having a clean slate just makes me feel like I've accomplished something! Then I went through all of the drawers to gather clothes we don't love and don't wear any more. It's amazing the things I held on to, "just in case." Those cases never came along, and now so many things I hold up and think to myself, there is no way I'm ever putting that thing on again!

As you go through your bedroom, try to make it a place where you can rest. Where you're not reminded of the things that need to be done. Buy yourself some new sheets or even some new candles. Make it a place you enjoy being, and a place you find peace.

Chapter 10

Living Spaces

Our living space is not only where we spend most of our time; it's where all of our guests spend their time too. It should be warm and inviting and feel like home. A place where everyone can kick back, put their feet up, and feel welcomed.

This can be extremely difficult with kids in the house because, let's face it, there will always be toys strewn all over the place. When my kids were younger I kept most of their toys in their room and a small basket of things in the living room. I didn't want them to ever feel like they couldn't play where guests were. It's their house too and I felt like they needed the freedom to be themselves wherever they were.

As I've mentioned before, the house we were living in at the time I wrote this book was extremely small. I was also homeschooling, so this added even more clutter to our living space. My home office, school room, dining area, and living room were all one space. And most days I just wanted to hide in a corner and pretend nothing was even there. But, that wouldn't fix anything so I had to be creative with how and where I stored things. And some things were just plain ugly. Like my printer sitting on a little file cabinet next to the dining table. Not something you're gonna see in any magazines any time soon, but I have to make do with what I've got.

I certainly needed to make sure that I was only keeping what we needed, used, and loved. If I wasn't getting rid of something, then it needed to be stored. We used storage boxes for a lot of the kids' school items and extra paper and books. I also used magazine file boxes for each of their curriculum so they could just grab theirs when it was time for school. Just small, simple things to help keep control of the endless amounts of stuff that was floating around.

Like with other areas of the home, I always started with the surfaces. Getting rid of picture frames I didn't love any more, candles that didn't light any more, and anything that wasn't important to me. Then, I hit the bookshelves.

I must admit I have a major addiction to buying books. I don't like reading digital versions unless I absolutely have to. I like to hold the book in my hands, and then I end up getting attached to it. It's my friend. I underline and dog ear the pages like it's going out of style! If I ever live in a house big enough, I'll keep every book I ever buy and have a library. But, until then, I've learned to be a big girl and sacrifice the ones that I know I won't ever read again.

Same goes with movies and music. If the movie is 10 years old and it's not a classic, it's probably time to let it go! I used Amazon to list my used books and movies. So simple and earned some extra money. If you don't want to spend the time listing, I'm sure a library would love your hand-me-downs or you could donate them to your local thrift store.

When I had gotten rid of all that I was going to, I rearranged what was left in the most space-efficient way. I keep one shelf and a small crate for the games we play most often. Any other games stay up in the kids' room. I have a wire basket with my Bible, journal, and books that I am currently reading on an end table so that it's there for me every morning. Just taking the time to really make our house and our belongings work for us has made a huge difference in our day-to-day lives. None of this is new; it's just using what we have and making it work for us. You need to look at your home and figure out what will work best. If that means rearranging furniture, moving things to a different room, or just getting rid of stuff, then do it.

Make your home yours. Don't worry about making it look like a Pinterest board. Let it tell your story and be a reflection of you and your family. Let it reflect a life well lived. When you've simplified your home, you feel so much peace. You have the time and energy to focus on your purpose and enjoy life instead of trying to keep up with a home that is always falling apart.

Home Assessment

On a scale of 1-10, how satisfied are you with your home?

_____

_____

What are some things you need to do to start moving towards being completely satisfied in this area?

_____

_____

_____

_____

What are some things you need to let go of in this area?

_____

_____

_____

_____

Home Highlights

Assess your home and come up with a goal.
Create a master task list.
Work in 15 minute increments.
If you don't love it and haven't used it, toss it.
Plan your menu one to two weeks in advance.
Wipe your sinks every day.
Do a load of laundry every day.

My favorite home resources can all be found at corieclark.com/simplicityresources or in my amazon shop at www.amazon.com/shop/corieclark

Section Three | Simplifying your finances

Chapter 11

Money, Money, Money

Oh, money. We'd all love to have just a little bit more, right? We think this would solve all of our problems. Until it does. And then we want just a little bit more.

Finding balance in the reasons we "want" money is very tricky. Wanting more money to "prove" we're better or above someone else is just wrong. Being able to afford nice things because we have worked hard and earned that money is totally ok. It ultimately comes down to living within our means and leaving some room for saving, giving, or just splurging once in a while.

> *For the love of money is the root of all kinds of evil.*
>
> 1 Timothy 6:10

Somewhere along the road, we've misinterpreted this verse and started believing that money is the root of all kinds of evil. This is so far from the truth. Money helps people. It provides shelter, food, and clothing. Money is not bad. It's not from the devil. It's necessary. It's the love of money that can lead to evil, not money itself.

So from this point forward, don't worry about earning money, or buying nice things. Every single person needs money. They need to earn money; they need to spend money; they need to save money. Don't feel guilty for dreaming and wanting to run a successful business. You were created to do something very specific and if you can make a living at it, then by all means go for it.

Too many times I've found myself feeling guilty for charging someone for the work I've done or for wanting to start a business. I even felt guilty for wanting to write this book! But the truth of the matter is that we shouldn't feel guilty for any of it. If you have worked hard and are living within your means, don't feel guilty for going on a vacation or buying a new outfit. Guilt is from the enemy. You're allowed to enjoy your life; in fact, you're supposed to!

Financial freedom will do so much more than send you on your next vacation. It will give the margin you need to live on purpose and help others. My husband and I always give, even when we have little. When you get yourself into the habit of giving, you will be amazed at the blessing that you receive for doing so. As you create this habit of giving, it will continue to grow as your income grows.

As we approach simplifying our finances and getting them in order, I dare you to dream. Dream big! Don't live with a poverty mentality that you have to live on nothing. Being willing to give everything up and living that lifestyle when you haven't been asked to are two very different things. So dream about your future. Dream about what you want to do with your life and how you want to be able to bless others. You have to have an end goal to keep you focused, or else you'll be headed nowhere fast.

A note from Corie: I am leaving the rest of this section on finances as I originally wrote it because this is where we were at the time. And if you're in need of simplifying, this is likely where you'll have to start as well. After going through this process of simplifying our lives and finances, we were able to build a successful business and have since made big shifts in our money mindset and how we handle our finances. We don't necessarily follow all of these rules any more but they were necessary at the time and helped us get out of what felt like a dire situation.

Chapter 12

Dream Big

We have so many preconceived ideas and beliefs around money and far too often those are the exact things that are keeping us from true financial freedom. Money is a tool and we must conquer our fears and misbeliefs around it so that we can actually start to use it the way God intended!

The first step in simplifying our finances and ultimately achieving financial freedom is getting to look at the big picture. Think about where you want to be in one year, five years, and ten years. Do you want to be debt free? Do you want to own a home? Do you want to take yearly vacations? Or maybe you're looking into retirement. Do you want to be able to retire without a care in the world other than where to go next in your RV? Think about the things that you want to be able to do. Now, write them down. Don't worry; they're not set in stone. You will most likely make changes every year, month, or even as much as every week if you're just beginning to take control of your finances. It's ok! Grace. That's all I can say. Grace for your mistakes, grace for your learning, grace for your dreams.

Here's what my big picture looks like.

In One Year

I want our debts completely gone. {We're already pretty close because we've been working on this for quite some time}.

I want to be able to take my kids on a family vacation paid for by cash.
I want to have a 3 month emergency fund.

In Five Years

I want to be in our own home.
I want to take yearly vacations.
I want to have a 6-month emergency fund.
I want to have a substantial amount put into our retirement fund.
I want a college fund for my children.

In Ten Years

I want to continue our family vacations.
I want to be able to pay for the kids' college.
I want to be able to pay for my daughter's wedding.
I want to be on the path to a fully funded retirement.

Now it's your turn. Dream big!

In One Year

_____
_____
_____
_____

In Five Years

_____
_____
_____
_____

In Ten Years

_____
_____
_____
_____

Now that you have your dreams out of your mind and onto paper, you can start breaking them down into small, achievable goals. For instance, if I want our debts completely gone, I need to have a grand total and divide it by twelve to be sure I can pay them off in twelve months. If I want to take my family on a $5,000 vacation, then I need to set a goal of saving around $425 per month. You get the idea. And this is where you will see if you need to adjust your goals.

Once you have the big picture in mind, it's time to figure out how to reach those goals. Can they be accomplished with your current income? Or do you need to make more money? Can you reach them by cutting out some expenses? You're only going to be able to figure these things out when you have a budget and stick to it. I know; easier said than done. Remain persistent and you'll see it all fall into place.

Chapter 13

The B Word

IF.... And that's a big IF! If your finances are in complete and utter chaos, then this is something that has to be done. It doesn't mean it has to be a way of life forever. But more often than not, we don't even know where our money is, how much we have, how much we spend, and how much we make.

If that sounds like you, which is where we once were, then this section is for you!

Before we even dive into this, I want you to take a deep breath and say this with me, "Budgets are not the devil." The word budget is not a bad word. It shouldn't make you cringe. It shouldn't make you shut down. Oh, I can't begin to tell you how much I hated the process of figuring out our budget. But it actually had nothing to do with us not having enough money. It was irritating to think of how much money we've wasted over the years on who knows what. We had to give ourselves grace. What's done is done. We can't go back. We can only move forward.

Creating a budget is an integral step if you want to simplify your finances. And no, checking your bank account every day is not a budget. Reconciling your account at the end of each month is not a budget either. A budget is a plan, before you even get your paycheck, on where exactly each and every dollar is going to go. This doesn't mean you don't get to have any fun; it just means that you are telling your money which is going to be spent on fun and which isn't. So for instance, if you want to go to the movies, put it in the budget.

If you're in a place where you are too scared to even look at your financial situation, like I was, I promise that it is much less scary once you have it written down on paper. You can try to figure it out in your mind until you're blue in the face. But you'll still miss something. WRITE. IT. DOWN.

Budgets can be good. They are a tool to help you and give you a framework for where you are. In fact, they can actually increase your income. Your paycheck may not go up, but I can almost guarantee you are going to find areas where you can spend less, thus, giving you more cash flow to allocate elsewhere. If you are married, this is definitely something you need to do with your spouse. You're a team and you need to figure out a way, together, how to reach your goals.

When my husband and I went through a finance class, we took a 10-question assessment to see if we were "Free Spirits" or "Nerds." The crazy thing is, I got six points for free spirit and four points for nerd, while my husband got four points for free spirit and six points for nerd. Now, you may be thinking to yourself that this is good because we're pretty middle of the road. Not so much. We actually don't fight a whole lot about money but what we do have working against us is the fact that we're both nerd enough to want to stick to the budget and we're both free spirit enough to say, "Oh, what the heck. Let's go out to dinner!" Not good, people. I'm glad we know this now, though, because we know it's an issue that needs to be addressed.

You may want to consider taking a similar assessment with your spouse. Or you may already know who the free spirit is and who the nerd is. Know that you're made different and use your differences to balance each other out.

The Baby Budget

When you start the process of budgeting, you're going to ease into it with a baby budget. If this is your first time actually writing out a budget, you're going to take a baby step. You probably have some sort of idea of how your money comes in and goes out. I want you to write it down. There's only one rule. You must come up with $0 at the end.

Here's an example:

Let's say your income is $5,000 for the month. Add up all of your expenses to a balance of $5000.

Income after taxes + $5,000

Giving (-$500)

Saving (-$500)

Housing (-$1,500)

Food (-$1,000)

Transportation (-$500)

Utilities (-$300)

Personal (-$700)

Total $0

Now it's your turn. Remember, this doesn't have to be perfect. This is just to get the wheels turning and you thinking about where your money is going. Again, make sure your total is $0.

Income after taxes _____

Giving _____

Saving _____

Housing _____

Food _____

Transportation _____

Utilities _____

Personal _____

Total _____

This step alone can be very eye-opening if you've never done this before. This will give you a good idea of what needs to be worked on so you can complete a detailed, zero balance budget going forward.

The Big Budget

Now that you have a very loose idea of where your money is going every month, it's time to get down to the nitty gritty. Once again, if you are married, this is something you need to do with your spouse. You both need to know where every dollar is going so that you can make decisions together on what changes need to be made. You will not get it down perfectly and you will probably argue. Give each other grace and remember that despite your differences, your goals are the same.

When my husband and I go through this process, we print out the last few bank statements so that we can go over them line by line and make sure we're not missing anything. We also need to be aware of what's coming up that month. If there are birthday parties, weddings, graduations, any kind of varied or extra expense, it needs to be budgeted. This big budget is going to list every expense. For example, instead of just a "Food" category, you'll split it into "Groceries" and "Dining Out."

Here are the most common categories. Again, you can print out your own form with the bonuses found in chapter 18.

Giving
Tithes
Offerings
Charity

Saving
Emergency
Retirement
College
Vacation

Housing
Rent/Mortgage
Taxes
Association
Maintenance

Food
Groceries
Dining Out

Utilities
Electricity
Gas
Water
Trash
Phone
Internet
Cable

Transportation
Insurance
Gas
License

Insurance
Life
Health
Homeowners

Leisure
Entertainment
Children's Sports

Personal
Nanny
Babysitting
Toiletries
Subscriptions
Supplies
Blow Money

Debts
Car Payments
Credit Cards
Personal Loans
Student Loans

Keep in mind that all of your expenses need to add up to your total take-home pay. If you're coming up short, you need to tighten the budget on things like leisure and food. If you have extra money, you can add it to paying down debt or building up savings. Be sure that every single dollar has a place to belong.

Chapter 14

Stretch that Green

Getting out of unnecessary debt might feel hard. But you know what? It's even harder when you keep adding to it. If this is a problem area for you, I cannot stress enough the importance of cutting up your credit cards even if it's just for a short period while you address the problem.

But what if? I know; it's scary. We never know what life will throw at us. Injury, sickness, flat tires, broken appliances, the list goes on. We know these things are going to happen, so it's our responsibility to be prepared. We may not ever be emotionally ready for some of life's unexpected moments. But at least we can be financially prepared to some extent.

This is why building an emergency fund is so important. This will come in handy and keep you from using your credit cards.

Try not to be discouraged if your money is stretched thin. My husband and I have had to rebuild this fund countless times. It's so hard when you're living paycheck to paycheck. And it seems like every time we get ahead, something else makes us fall behind. This has been the story of our lives for the past 17 years. But I can honestly say, I'd rather be at this point than drowning in hundreds of thousands of dollars of debt. At least we're in control and slowly creeping towards our goal and not away from it.

If this is how you feel, just know there's hope. I believe you can find things to cut out of your budget that you wouldn't normally give a second thought to. If you truly can't find anything at all to cut out of your budget, then you're going to have to get creative with how you build this fund. You will have to find ways to earn the money.

If you're feeling defeated and like hope is lost, remember that you do have control of your money. I know there are times that it feels like you don't and that you're a sinking ship but if you just step back and get creative, you can find ways to save and ways to earn. Still at a loss? Let's go over some budget saving and money earning ideas.

Money Saving Tips

1. Give up eating out and entertainment for a month or two.
2. Have a menu plan to avoid last minute drive-thrus.
3. Make your own meals at home. Live on rice and beans for a while if you have to.
4. Cut up and freeze produce that's about to go bad. Use for smoothies later.
5. Make your own baby food.
6. Drink more water. Juices and soft drinks are very pricey.
7. Make your own coffee.
8. Refrigerate leftover coffee for iced coffee later.
9. Cook and eat what's in season.
10. Buy in bulk.
11. Scour grocery ads for the best deals. Stock up when items are at their lowest.
12. Use coupons.
13. Stick to the list. If it's not on your list, don't buy it.
14. Buy dried beans instead of canned.
15. Avoid processed foods. Pound for pound they are more expensive than fruits and veggies.
16. Eat leftovers.
17. Pack your lunch.

18. Take a snack and water with you when you leave the house.
19. Sign up for rewards programs at the stores you shop most.
20. Buy store brand.
21. Stop buying water bottles. Get a filter and use your own reusable bottles.
22. Grow your own veggies and herbs.
23. Use cash for everyday purchases. You'll stick to your budget better.
24. Plan all of your errands in one day to avoid extra driving.
25. Make your own cleaning supplies.
26. Make your own face wash.
27. Use rags or washcloths instead of paper towels.
28. Use cloth napkins instead of paper.
29. Don't use paper plates.
30. Keep your lights off when you don't need them.
31. Unplug electronics that aren't in use.
32. Cancel cable.
33. Adjust your thermostat by a degree or two when using your heater or air.
34. Take shorter showers.
35. Wash your clothes in cold water.
36. Shop at thrift stores.
37. Do a clothing swap with friends to give yourself a new wardrobe.
38. Make your own gifts.
39. Use Rakuten to earn cash back on your online purchases.
40. Comparison shop. Amazon is usually cheaper and get free shipping with Amazon Prime.
41. Wait 24-48 hours when deciding on a big purchase.
42. Cancel your gym membership.
43. Cancel other memberships that you rarely use {Spa, book clubs, etc}
44. Use the library.
45. Carpool.

46. Ride your bike or walk.
47. Cancel a phone line or combine services.
48. Compare car insurance rates.
49. Subscribe to the magazines you must have instead of buying at the store.
50. Trade services with friends. {Baby-sitting, etc.}

Buying in Bulk

Buying in bulk is a great way to save quite a bit of money, but only if you use the products you buy before they go bad, and if the cost per item or ounce is actually less than when purchased in a regular size. So, there's no sense in spending $20 on peanut butter if it's going to take you six months to eat it. Buy the $3 jar of peanut butter and use the extra $17 for something else. We only shop at a club store for items that will be used within two weeks.

You also need to be sure that the cost of a membership to a club store is going to be worth it. You should be able to more than pay for it in your savings, so if you only go a couple of times a year, it may not be worth it. If you do want to join a big club store, but don't want to spend a lot on membership, consider going in on the membership with a friend. You can also do joint shopping trips and split items that you may not need as much of to get the discounted price.

Couponing

Couponing is wonderful because it's basically free money. When I used to print my coupons it was kind of like printing my own money, and it was legal! Of course now, they're all in our grocery store apps but they still work just the same!

I used to be a coupon queen. I still love coupons and use them regularly, but in order to simplify my life, I needed to cut out some of the time I was spending on it. If you have the time, it is so worth it. You can save hundreds of dollars every month if you do it right.

Couponing will work best when you stack a coupon with a rock bottom price. Even better when you earn store rewards at the same time. When this happens, you need to stock up on that item so you don't have to pay full price when you run out.

Stick to one or two stores, scour the ads, and keep your coupons with you. Many stores will let you use one manufacturer's coupon and one store coupon per item. This is where the savings really add up. If this is something that you have time for, I highly suggest doing it. There are several couponing blogs that I highly recommend. I'll list them later in the resource section for your reference.

Making Your Own Cleaning and Personal Supplies

Making your own cleaning and personal care items is a great way to save money and cut out the chemicals that you use. There are only 2 things that I personally take the time to make. Multi-purpose cleaner and face wash. If I'm simplifying, I don't want to spend a ton of time making things that I can buy for a fairly decent price. I would love to make my own laundry detergent, deodorant, lotion, and more, but it's just not the right time for me. If you have the time and need to save money, these are great ways to do it.

Canceling Cable

We've lived without cable for about 5 years and we are doing just fine! We use Hulu and Netflix and invested in a digital antenna to watch local channels. We also have an Amazon Prime membership which we pay on an annual basis that includes tons of free movies and TV shows. We're spending less than $20 per month on our Hulu and Netflix memberships which is far less than the average cable bill. We could probably get rid of one of those, but there are certain things that the kids like that aren't on one or the other so for now we're keeping both.

Shopping Online

This wasn't quite as common back when I first wrote this book but I still want to emphasize it because the time and energy you save by ordering groceries and necessities equates to savings!

I do a huge amount of our shopping online. Especially during the holidays. Not only does it save me money, it saves time and headaches too. Most companies offer free returns and, it sure is easier to compare prices sitting at home than running around town. Amazon seems to offer the best prices overall and is a great site for comparison shopping.

Chapter 15

Bring Home the Bacon

Now that you know how much money is coming in and how much is going out, you might have realized you need more cash flow. Maybe you've stretched your budget as far as you possibly can and you're still not making enough.

When I first wrote this book, we really didn't have a ton of expenses other than the necessities. We didn't have credit card payments and we didn't have loans. Even so, we were still barely getting by. This meant we had a cash flow problem!

We learned to get creative with ways to bring in more income. We sold things, started businesses, worked side jobs...you name it. If this is your situation, then it's time for you to get creative and bring in some extra cash.

Here are some ideas of how to get cash in your pocket ASAP:
- Sell furniture you don't love or need.
- Sell electronics you can live without.
- Sell gold, silver, or jewelry.
- Sell clothing to second hand stores.
- Sell books, DVDs, CDs.
- Offer to sell other people's items for a fee.
- Take on babysitting jobs.
- Pet sit.
- Walk dogs.

- Start a paper route.
- Deliver pizzas.
- Mow lawns.
- Wash windows.
- Wash cars.
- Run errands.
- Clean homes.
- Start an odd jobs business.
- Make items to sell like candles or soap.
- Join a direct sales company.
- Write an eBook in your own area of expertise and sell it online
- The possibilities are endless in this digital age.

When it comes down to it, you can find a way to make money. How much money you will make is dependent on how much work you're willing to put in to go the extra mile. If you're willing to sacrifice for a little while and take on a second job or some side work, you'll be better for it in the end. You'll pay down your debt quicker and build up your emergency fund. It's amazing what a little blood, sweat, and tears will get you.

Stay Green

Using cash instead of your debit card plays a very important role in keeping to the budget. Full disclosure: I am horrible at this! I always have the best intentions of using cash and then for some reason I'll find myself swiping my debit card. Then I'll plan on getting out cash less the amount I just spent. And then I'll use the debit card again. And again. Mercy.

When we do pull out our cash on Fridays, after my husband has been paid, we are so much better at sticking to the budget. We use the envelope method we learned in a finance class, which truly does keep us from over spending. We usually only use it for groceries, gas, entertainment, and miscellaneous expenses. Anything that is automatic or paid online stays in the account, which is a huge help. But when you hold that cash in your hand and have to give it to the cashier, something happens in your brain that makes you think twice about what you are spending it on.

When working with a budget, anything that is automatic or paid online stays in the account. Anything you pay for in person should be paid in cash. Divide this cash into envelopes and label each one with the appropriate category. If you have $200 for groceries, then that's all you get to spend. End of story. Don't borrow from other envelopes. Stick to the plan. If you have left over cash at the end of the month you can either roll it over to the same category, put it in savings or toward debt, or splurge on something for yourself. If you consistently have an overage in a certain category then you should probably revise your budget and allocate that money to a different category.

Pay It Off

Once you've established your budget and you're living within your means, you should be able to rid yourself of the debt in no time. We started with the smallest debt, working our way up. If you've allotted yourself $500 per month to go towards paying off your debt, then you'd pay the minimum on your higher balances and put the rest towards the smallest one in order to completely pay that off as quickly as possible. As soon as that smallest debt is paid, you'll be able to apply what you were paying on it to the next in line along with what you are already paying. With every debt that gets paid, you'll have more and more to apply to the next one. Allowing you to pay them off quicker.

When your credit cards and loans are paid, you will feel a freedom that I can't explain. But I promise, it's worth the pain and sacrifice.

Save It

Once your debts are paid, you can start saving. It's a good idea to have six months of expenses set aside for an emergency. Do you know what you'll do if you or your spouse loses your job? If you get sick or injured? If you have six months of expenses saved, you'll be able to breathe a little and focus on what your next step will be. This doesn't need to be six months of the lifestyle you're living now, just six months of the bare minimum to get by.

As you start to apply these concepts, you'll realize that money, or the lack thereof, doesn't have to rule you because you have complete control over your financial situation. Once you're out of debt and are saving up your money, you'll be building wealth and living the life you've always dreamed.

Finance Highlights

Dream.
Set goals.
Make a budget.
Use cash.
Be creative with saving and earning.
Pay off debt.
Save.

My favorite finance resources can all be found at corieclark.com/simplicityresources

Section Four | Simplifying Your Time

Chapter 16

Time is on Your Side

Would you believe me if I told you that time is on your side? It is! I promise. Of course it can work completely against you if you let it, but just as we learned with money, if you tell it where to go, it'll work for you.

I can't tell you how many times I've gotten frustrated with myself for wasting time. Including, but not limited to, the 4 million times I got angry at myself for wasting time instead of writing this book! So, if you're holding this book in your hand, it's proof that you can take control of your time and get things done! We just have to learn how to tell our time where to go and then stay disciplined to our plan. And then we need to give ourselves grace when we occasionally waste time, because this will happen. And ain't nobody got time for beating ourselves up over wasted time! That's a surefire way to waste an entire day, week, months, or even worse, years.

I would have never dreamed a year ago that I would have had the time to homeschool my kids, maintain our home, take care of all of my wife and mommy duties, keep up with a blog, and write a book. But, what I came to realize is that we all have the exact same amount of hours every day and how I spend mine is completely my responsibility.

Truth: I still waste time. I still get frustrated. It takes work; it takes planning; and it takes discipline. But I am living proof that the time is there--it just needs to be used carefully and intentionally. It's time to start using your time to live the life you've always wanted.

Eliminate The Distractions

We are quite the busy society aren't we? Our phones are on our nightstand and we check them immediately when we open our eyes in the morning. We check our emails, notifications, see who's doing what and where on all of our social media outlets, then hit the ground running. Gotta work out, make breakfasts, make lunches, get the kids out the door, check the phone again, reply to emails, work, study, check the phone again, do some laundry, check the phone, clean the house, check the phone, meet friends for coffee, make that dentist appointment, pick up the kids, drive them all over town to the latest and greatest sports practice, check the phone again, run to the grocery store, drive through some nasty fast-food joint because you're just too tired to even think about cooking, check homework, rush kids off to bed, check the phone again, plop on the couch and flip on the television. Phew! That made me tired just thinking about the things that have to get done on any given day. *Amiright?*

How many times a day, out of habit, do you check your phone? Can we please just get off these things? The amount of time wasted on those little handheld devices is astounding. Believe me, I am preaching to myself here. When we use our phones we can easily become addicted. Sure, it ain't real crack, alcohol, or pornography, but it rips us away from what's really important to us--our families, our dreams, and our purpose. Consider where those precious moments can be better spent the next time you reach for that little life-sucker.

Say No, So You Can Say Yes

Besides being distracted, we are an entirely over-committed generation. From jobs to school, church to sports, we just can't.say.no.

For a long period of time I was burning the candle at both ends. I was trying to homeschool the kids, keep up with the house, maintain a blog, write a book, and serve at church several times a week. I had to step back and look at what I was really called to do and what I was actually doing just because I thought it was the right thing to do. Please understand, just because something is a good cause doesn't mean you have to be involved.

Likewise, your kids don't need to participate in every sport and activity just because they'd have fun. Do fewer things and do them well. I fully believe that God graces you for the work He's called you to do. This doesn't mean all of the work that others have called you to do. Use discernment and learn to say no. If it's what you're supposed to be doing it will work out.

Saying no to friends has always been extremely hard for me. Since I'm such a free spirit, my first instinct is to say yes to any request or offer. This is still a work in progress for me, and I have to be careful to weigh my other responsibilities before I commit. I love to help people out; if I've been diligent with my time management and I'm not going, going, going, 24 hours a day, then I have margin to drop what I'm doing and help them out. If you're being stretched in too many directions, you need to ask yourself what things are taking you down the path that fulfills your purpose and follows your dreams. If something is pulling you away from that, then maybe it's time to let go.

Routine

Creating a simple morning and evening routine will help you to establish good habits. I started small with just three tasks in the morning and three tasks in the evening. I printed them out and taped them to my mirror to remind me. After a few weeks these things become routine and now I hardly even think about doing them. Once you've established a small routine, you can add a couple of tasks to each one. I don't suggest more than five because we don't want to be robots, right? But some routine is good and helps us stay on track with the things that just have to get done.

Here's what my routines look like:

Morning
Coffee
Bible
Laundry
Write

Evening
Start dishwasher
Straighten kitchen
Look over tomorrow's schedule
Wash face / Brush teeth

Here are some practical things you can do to help you get a better handle on your time. Some of these things we do without even noticing and they waste so much time.

25 Time Saving Tips

1. Track your time for a few days. Write down what you're doing every fifteen minutes so you can get an idea of how you spend your time.
2. Get up early! Especially if you have kids. I know, it's so hard. But, the amount of things I get done before my kids get up is astounding.
3. Limit your television time. You probably watch more than you think.
4. Limit your internet surfing time. If you don't set a timer, you can spend hours online without even realizing it.
5. Set a timer when browsing social media sites.
6. Create email filters.
7. Unsubscribe from email lists that don't interest you. It will only take about ten seconds longer than just deleting it, and then you won't be bothered with it any more.

8. Delete apps that waste your time. You know the ones!
9. Plan your menu one to two weeks out.
10. Spend ten minutes meeting with your family at the beginning of the week to go over everyone's plans and the menu. This will save lots of questions and keep everyone on the same page.
11. Prep as much as you can the night before. Backpacks, lunches, sweatshirts.
12. Plan errands around each other.
13. Shop online.
14. Keep a shopping list on the fridge to write down items you need as soon as you run out.
15. Wear clothes more than once if they're not dirty.
16. Establish a morning and evening routine.
17. Cook double the amount and eat leftovers or freeze for later.
18. Use a slow cooker or pressure cooker
19. Prep smoothie freezer bags.
20. Do one load of laundry everyday, no matter what. This will help you avoid the five load days.
21. Keep a laundry sorter in the laundry room so the laundry is presorted and you can just toss the laundry in and go.
22. Do quick, five-minute, clean-ups throughout the day to keep things from getting out of control.
23. Wipe down all of your counters every day so you don't have to deep clean as often.
24. Give the kids chores {and pay them}. They need to learn the value of work and it will take some of the load off of you.
25. Multi-task. {I listen to books on Audible or podcasts while I walk.}

Chapter 17

Budget Your Time

Have you ever met someone and wondered how in the world they do it all? Like the executive working sixty hours a week who still manages to start side businesses, take family vacations, and go to their children's sporting events. Or the mom who makes every craft in the book, cooks every meal from scratch, harvests vegetables from their own garden, and hosts a moms' group every week in their perfectly clean home? You know, the kind of people you look at and think, if only I could get it together like that person. Or, if only I had enough extra time on my hands to start a new business or take a side job to pay some bills. They must have some sort of super power, right? Probably not. They're likely just budgeting their time and using it wisely.

Think of your time like you would your checking account. With a budget, you know how much money you'll have in the month and you know where it will all go by the end of the month. Technically, we also know exactly how much time we'll have each month, each week, and each day. You just need to tell it where to go instead of wondering where it went.

As soon as you start to treat time in the same way that you treat money, you'll realize you have more time than you think. In fact, you may find yourself being one of those ambitious entrepreneurs or that super mom you thought just had super powers.

Define Your Roles

The first thing you need to do to start budgeting your time is to define your roles. Who are you? What do you want to do or be? What do you need to do to fulfill your purpose and live out your dreams?

In Stephen Covey's book, First Things First[2], he tells a story of a lecture that one of his associates sat in on. The lecturer pulled out a jar and filled it with fist sized stones. It was full. Then the lecturer added gravel which filled in all of the empty gaps between the larger rocks. Now it was full. Then, the lecturer proceeded to fill the jar with sand, which filled the even smaller holes. And, finally, he filled it with water. Had he done these things in reverse order, he never would have been able to fit the big stones in.

The point being, you need to make sure you take care of the big stones first. When you do, everything else can be filled in between. Your main roles are your big stones.

My four main roles are:
1. Child of God
2. Wife
3. Mom
4. Business Owner

Write down your four most important roles.

_____

_____

_____

_____

Next, decide what things you need to do or want to do to be the best you possibly can at each role.

Here's what I came up with:

Child of God
- Attend church
- Daily time with God
- Serve others
- Tend to relationships

Wife
- Spend time alone with Ryan
- Date night at least twice a month
- Keep our home running smoothly

Mom
- Spend one on one time with the kids
- Homeschool three days per week
- Play games and read with them

Business Owner
- Create content every day
- Engage with my community every day
- Read books every day

Now, it's your turn. Write down your roles and things that you need to do to make you better at them.

Role #1 _____

_____

_____

_____

Role #2 _____

_____

_____

_____

Role #3_____

_____

_____

_____

Role #4 _____

_____

_____

Now, look at your weekly planner, and fill in your big stones. These are things that you absolutely can't get around, like church, school, and work. You can fill in your sleep time too if you want. When I make my weekly schedule I fill in these things first: Church, serving, date night, school, sports, and my work.

Next, start filling in the gaps with the actionable items that you wrote under your roles. This should be done with pencil because I guarantee it's not going to work out the first time you try this. Are there things you've been working on that deserve less priority? Or do you have more time than you thought you did? Make your time work for you and tell it where to go. Don't wonder where it went at the end of every day!

When I first went through this process, I scheduled everything to the half hour. I included drive time to and from school and my daughter's ballet class. I really tried to make sure I wasn't leaving anything out. If I only wrote in her 2-hour class, it wouldn't be realistic. I am gone for three hours when I include my drive time. I don't live each day scheduled to the half hour but to get a good idea of how to take control of my time, I had to write down everything.

Here's an example of one of my days from when I wrote the book and the kids were younger. And, no, I didn't follow this to the minute every day. It's just a guide and can change as your life changes!

6:00 Wake up and make coffee

6:15 Bible/Journal

6:45 Read

7:00 Wake kids and make lunches

7:30 Breakfast

8:00 Leave for homeschool charter

8:40 Home and look over to do list

8:45 Start Laundry and clean up kitchen

9:15 Write/Blog/Work

10:15 Work out

11:00 Lunch

11:30 Shower

12:30 Work on blog or other tasks from to-do list

1:15 Prep for dinner

1:45 Leave to pick up kids

2:30 Home

3:00 Leave for ballet

6:00 Home/Dinner

7:00 Clean up

7:30 Play a game

8:00 Kids get ready for bed

9:00 Alone time with Ryan

11:00 Bedtime

Now that I've gotten used to my schedule, I can fill out a weekly plan at the beginning of each week to get a bird's eye view of what the family is up to. Then, I set a daily plan each night for the following day. My weekly plan only has the big stones and appointments so I can easily check my schedule with a quick glance.

My daily plan is divided into the following sections (and this is how the Purposeful Planner came to be):

Top 3 - The three most important things that need to be done that day. These are things that I need to do to reach a goal or work on my dreams and purpose. Anything that I don't get finished is carried over to the next day.

Hourly schedule

Brain Dump - This is for anything I need to do or think of throughout the day. Tasks that need to be done but aren't necessarily in my top three.

Dinner Menu - I fill in this section at the beginning of the week.

Health - This is where I track my exercise and water intake.

Retail Therapy - This is where I jot down things that need to be bought. Not a full grocery list but if I remember the kids need new socks or a birthday present that needs to be purchased.

This is what works for me and it might be right for you too. Remember, we're simplifying, not complicating. We're creating margin in our schedules to have room for God to move and for us to achieve our dreams and live out our purpose. We're not creating margin to add more to the to-do list.

Having a plan and writing it down will save you tons of time. Figure out what will work for you and for your family. Getting into this habit creates discipline and you will be more inclined to plan things you want to do and less inclined to waste time on trivial things

Time Highlights

Put the phone down.
Say no more often.
Know your roles.
Budget your time.

My favorite time resources can all be found at corieclark.com/simplicityresources

Section Five | Simplicity Now

Chapter 18

Bringing it All Together

As you can see, each of the key areas we have discussed are actually woven together. When we are disciplined and take care of ourselves first, we have the energy to take care of our families and homes. We aren't exhausted and we can actually think clearly enough to make a plan, keep our homes peaceful, feed ourselves good food, stick to a budget, and do things that matter.

As I've lived this project, as I've toiled, cried, prayed, and screamed, I've learned that it's so worth it. I'm not perfect. I've probably learned more about giving myself grace while going through this project than I ever have before.

A life of simplicity can truly be achieved if you commit to it and stay disciplined. I pray that this book has helped you realize some things about yourself and given you hope that you don't have to live a life of chaos and clutter. I pray that you learn to dream again. I pray that you find your purpose. I pray that you love this life.

We were created to live a life of purpose and it's our responsibility to take action in it. Life is good. Let's not waste another moment on something that is meaningless.

* Bonus Content *

As the owner of this book, you are entitled to some great bonuses! Go to corieclark.com/SPB

You'll get:
- Exclusive access to The Simplicity Project private Facebook group for support, ideas, and encouragement.
- The 28-Day Simplicity Project sent directly to your inbox each morning.
- Printables to help you in each area that was covered in this book.

28 Day Simplicity Project

Some of us have created bad habits of clutter and chaotic living over the years that need to be broken. They didn't develop overnight so they're not going to get fixed overnight. I can't even promise that it will happen in twenty-eight days. But what I have come up with is a plan to set you on the path to simplicity. It changed my life and I believe it can change yours too.

For those of you who are overwhelmed, hopeless, and don't even know where to start, this is for you.

For the next twenty-eight days, we are going to attack the chaos in all four areas of our lives that were addressed in this book. At the end of the twenty-eight days, if you do everything that I ask you to, you are going to feel like you have room to breathe again. You may need to go through the twenty-eight days again. Or maybe you'll have to go through it several times. But, I can promise that you will make progress and have the freedom to start living your life on purpose. The way you were created to and the way you want to.

You may want to get an accountability partner. Someone who understands you and has similar things that need to be addressed in their lives too. If you're married, let your spouse know what you're doing and let them be part of the journey.

Before you dive in head first, I want you to look through each of these days to get an idea of what's ahead. I have put them in a certain order because some tasks need to be done before others. This doesn't mean you can't make this your own and adjust it. Just browse through each one so you know what's coming. This way, if you know you're going to be gone for an entire day and won't be able to complete that day's task, you can double up the day before or the day after.

I also added days that aren't completely task-driven and focus more on you. So don't worry about burning out. That's not gonna happen. This was created to simplify your life, not complicate it.

Most of these tasks will only take you fifteen minutes. If you're a mama of little ones, then you may need to split it into two shorter sessions or wait until they're napping. We all know that no mother in the history of ever can go fifteen minutes without being interrupted! If you have more time on your hands and can spend more time on the tasks, I suggest not spending more than an hour on something. You may end up burnt out and not want to do the next day's task.

Most importantly, give yourself grace. If you miss a day, just pick up where you left off. No need to try and catch up. Face the problem head on, one step at a time. Let's get this done!

Day 1

Let's Do This!

Today you're going to take an assessment of your life and your home. If you haven't done so yet, write down what you want your life to look like in the next year and the next five years.

Then, write down how you want your home to feel and look. We covered these in section 2.

Next, you're going to do your walk through and make a master list of all of the tasks needed to simplify your home. This will be used over the next twenty-eight days as a guide to make sure that you're not forgetting anything. It will also be what you refer to if you don't need to do one of the tasks that I assign. If there ever is a day during the 28-day challenge that you have already done the task or you have time to tackle more, spend fifteen minutes tackling something on this master list.

You may want to tape this somewhere you will always see it. Be sure to let your family know that they are more than welcome to help get some things checked off that list too!

Cheers!
Corie
xox

PS. When you're done with this challenge, post a picture on instagram tagging me @corieclark and using the hashtag #simplicityproject

Day 2

Quick Purge

Today, take a walk through your house with one trash bag and two large boxes. This is not a go-through-every-cabinet-and-drawer mission. This is a quick walk through each room of the house throwing away anything and everything that belongs in the garbage. Broken toys, partially burned candles, single socks that have lost their partner.... Fill one box with anything you don't want anymore but doesn't need to be added to the landfill. These are items that you will donate to a shelter or local thrift store. The second box is for items that you want to sell.

If you're not in the mood to list things or have a garage sale, then just donate these too. If you haven't used it in a long time or you just don't love it, then get rid of it!

When you're done, take the trash out immediately and put the donation box in the trunk of your car to drop off the next time you're out. If you have a "sell" box, put it in a convenient area of your home where you can add to it. Let your family know it's there too. They can add items they want to sell as well. You'll hopefully find a lot more to sell over the next couple of weeks.

Cheers!
Corie
xox

PS. When you're done with this challenge, post a picture on instagram tagging me @corieclark and using the hashtag #simplicityproject

Day 3

Move It

Today you are going to take care of YOU. I want you to go on a 20-minute walk {or longer if you have the time and energy}. Get your heart pumping and your mind turning. A walk can be so beneficial for many reasons. You'll burn calories, have time alone, get some fresh air, and maybe even have a few ideas of how you can live your life on purpose. Let yourself dream a little while you're out there.

When you get back, tackle something on your master list. This can be a task of your choosing that will take less than fifteen minutes.

Cheers!
Corie
xox

PS. When you're done with this challenge, post a picture on instagram tagging me @corieclark and using the hashtag #simplicityproject

Day 4

Clear Those Counters

Today, spend fifteen minutes clearing your kitchen and bathroom counters. Don't worry about deep cleaning, this is just making space. If there are items taking up counter space that you don't use on a daily basis, find a home for them. Just clearing some space on the counters will help you to feel like you have more room and less clutter. The less you have to look at, the more free your mind will feel too.

Cheers!
Corie
xox

PS. When you're done with this challenge, post a picture on instagram tagging me @corieclark and using the hashtag #simplicityproject

Day 5

Bye Bye Clothes

Today, fill a trash bag with clothes you don't want or wear any more. I don't care if you've never worn an item and there are still tags on it. Get rid of the clothes. Not only will you be freeing up space in your closet, you'll be getting rid of the guilt that comes along with not wearing something that you've bought or been given. This doesn't have to be a long process.

Set your timer for fifteen minutes and fill that bag! If you get through the closet in less than fifteen minutes, move to your dresser or another closet.

If you're feeling motivated and have the time, head to the kid's room and set your timer for fifteen more minutes!

Cheers!
Corie
xox

PS. When you're done with this challenge, post a picture on instagram tagging me @corieclark and using the hashtag #simplicityproject

Day 6

Emergency!

Do you have an emergency fund? No?! Then today is your day. You are going to come up with a plan to get that emergency fund. Find room in your budget, sell something, do what you need to do to get $1,000 set aside. Most people can find a way to fund this in less than two weeks. Mark your calendar and try to beat it!

Cheers!
Corie
xox

PS. When you're done with this challenge, post a picture on instagram tagging me @corieclark and using the hashtag #simplicityproject

Day 7

It's All About You

I want you to choose a special place for your personal time. This could be a favorite comfy chair or a quiet room in your home. Prep it for your "me time." Set out your Bible, journal, other books, pens, and a candle. In my home I have a little basket that holds my Bible, journal, and books that I'm currently reading. Make your space a place that you want to be and commit to spending more time there.

Now, I want you to set a timer and read for thirty minutes. Yes, thirty minutes. Whether it's a book you've been putting off reading or just some good old fashioned tabloid magazine. Let yourself rest and read for thirty minutes. Once again, if you're a mama of little ones, save this time for when they're napping or down for the night so that you can enjoy a complete thirty minutes!

Cheers!
Corie
xox

PS. When you're done with this challenge, post a picture on instagram tagging me @corieclark and using the hashtag #simplicityproject

Day 8

How's Your Health?

Today, make a commitment to improve your health. What's one thing you can do consistently for the next three weeks?

Here are some ideas:
- Give up sugar
- Give up processed foods
- Give up soda
- Eat more veggies
- Eat clean
- Exercise more

Write down your goal and stick it on your fridge or somewhere that you will be reminded of it daily. Better yet, leave it a few places like the front door and the bathroom mirror to keep it fresh in your mind. Tell a friend or your spouse and ask them to join you in the commitment.

You need someone to keep you accountable and it sure makes the job a little less painful when you have someone going through it with you.

Now, spend fifteen minutes purging your pantry and fridge. Toss anything that isn't going to be eaten or is expired. Toss the junk too. If it's not there, you won't eat it. If you have items that are unopened and not expired, donate them to your local food bank. Giving your pantry an overhaul is going to put you on the path to wellness.

Cheers!
Corie
xox

PS. When you're done with this challenge, post a picture on instagram tagging me @corieclark and using the hashtag #simplicityproject

Day 9

Kitchen Purge

Today, you're tackling the kitchen. I want you to purge your kitchen drawers and cabinets.

This does not have to be a drawn out process. No perfectionism allowed. Open each cabinet and drawer one at a time and grab the items that you immediately recognize as a waste of space. The kitchen loves to collect gadgets and gizmos by the ton and most of them never get used! Put these items in a donation box or a sell box for a garage sale. If you have small appliances that are in good condition, you can list them on a local online marketplace too.

Cheers!
Corie
xox

PS. When you're done with this challenge, post a picture on instagram tagging me @corieclark and using the hashtag #simplicityproject

Day 10

Do You Know Where Your Money Went?

Today, you're going to make your quick budget. Remember, this doesn't have to be perfect.

This is to get a good idea of how much money you have coming in and going out each month. You're going to start telling your money where to go instead of wondering where it went at the end of each month. Do this the old-fashioned way. Grab a pencil and paper and start crunching numbers.

If you are married then this is something you need to do with your spouse. Set aside time to meet alone and go over the numbers. If you're busy like most married couples, one of you can get prepped by having your known numbers {like income, mortgage, loan payments, and insurance} ready to go and then when you meet, you can discuss how much you will budget for the more flexible expenses like savings, food, and entertainment.

Cheers!
Corie
xox

PS. When you're done with this challenge, post a picture on instagram tagging me @corieclark and using the hashtag #simplicityproject

Day 11

What's For Dinner?

Today, you're going to make a list of twenty of your family's favorite meals. Then, make a well stocked pantry and fridge list of the items you need on hand for all of those meals. Be sure to include your favorite breakfast and lunch items in your pantry list.

Now that you have that list, plan your dinner menu for the next seven days. And remember, it's ok to include a date or take out night in that menu!

Cheers!
Corie
xox

PS. When you're done with this challenge, post a picture on instagram tagging me @corieclark and using the hashtag #simplicityproject

Day 12

Heading Down Under

Today you are going to de-clutter under all of your sinks.

This means the kitchen sink and all bathroom sinks. Grab any half used bottles that are never going to be used and toss them. That shampoo you had to try but didn't love, toss. The cleaning product that promised you a sparkly bathroom but failed to deliver, gone. All those little samples that you've been saving for God knows what, those are gone too! If you have any products that are unused and you know you won't use them in the future, donate them to your local women's shelter.

And please, check your bottles for any special instructions on disposal of chemicals. No need for anyone to break the law!

Cheers!
Corie
xox

PS. When you're done with this challenge, post a picture on instagram tagging me @corieclark and using the hashtag #simplicityproject

Day 13

Routine

Today you are going to set a morning and evening routine. All you have to do is write down three things you will do every morning and three things you will do every evening to make your day flow better. Tape them up in your bathroom or somewhere you'll see them every morning and every night.

Now, set your timer for fifteen minutes and tackle something on your master list.
Cheers!
Corie
xox

PS. When you're done with this challenge, post a picture on instagram tagging me @corieclark and using the hashtag #simplicityproject

Day 14

Rest That Bod

Today I want you to rest. No special tasks. Do something to pamper yourself. Read a book, take a bath, go for a stroll. Find something you don't normally take the time for and do it.

Cheers!
Corie
xox

PS. When you're done with this challenge, post a picture on instagram tagging me @corieclark and using the hashtag #simplicityproject

Day 15

What Time Is It?

In order to start working on your time, today you are going to write down your roles and what you need to do to fill those roles. Take a sheet of paper and divide it into four sections.

Write down your four main roles on this page. Then, write down three actionable things you need or want to do, in each section, to make you your best at each of these roles.

Now, I want you to look at your planner, and fill in the big stones that we talked about in the "Time" section of the book. These are things that you absolutely can't get around, like church, school, and work. Next, start filling in the gaps with the actionable items that you wrote under your roles. This should be done with pencil because I guarantee it's not going to work out the first time you try this.

Are there things that you've been working on that deserve less priority? Or do you have more time than you thought you did? Make your time work for you and tell it where to go. Don't wonder where it went at the end of every day!

Cheers!
Corie
xox

PS. When you're done with this challenge, post a picture on instagram tagging me @corieclark and using the hashtag #simplicityproject

Day 16

File Away

Today you will create a filing system that works for you. If you already have one that doesn't need fixing then you can just update your files. Make sure you've gotten rid of papers you don't need any more; shred any documents that have personal information.

You don't need a fancy file cabinet or hanging folders for that matter. I use 9x12 envelopes stored in a plastic file box. This saves me from accidentally shoving a paper in the wrong file or letting something fall out. I write the name of the file at the top of the envelope in thick black marker so that I can quickly spot them and then I file them alphabetically. Is this the only way? Absolutely not. That's why I encourage you to find a system that works for you.

Nothing is worse than needing an important document and not knowing where in the world it is. Don't ask me how I know this.

Cheers!
Corie
xox

PS. When you're done with this challenge, post a picture on instagram tagging me @corieclark and using the hashtag #simplicityproject

Day 17

Toss That Paper

{Err... I mean, Recycle}

If you're anything like me, you've got random papers scattered throughout your house. Receipts you don't need any more, ticket stubs, expired coupons, junk mail...you name it.

Today you are going to gather every piece of paper around your home that is not in a home. Put it all in one pile and don't walk away from it until it's gone. Recycle as much of it as you possibly can. If it needs to be filed, file it now. If it's a keepsake from one of your children, find a place to store it and put it there.

Believe me, I know this one can be difficult. I homeschool my three kids, run a home business, and live in a 1,200 square foot condo. If anyone has paper coming out of their ears, it's me!

Cheers!
Corie
xox

PS. When you're done with this challenge, post a picture on instagram tagging me @corieclark and using the hashtag #simplicityproject

Day 18

Show Time!

Today's the day I want you to purge your DVDs (and CDs if you still have them)! You'll probably have a good laugh at some of the movies and music you've held on to for so long. Things like this get outdated pretty quickly and can possibly be sold on a local marketplace app. If you're not up for pricing and posting, just donate them!

Cheers!
Corie
xox

PS. When you're done with this challenge, post a picture on instagram tagging me @corieclark and using the hashtag #simplicityproject

Day 19

Are You Reading That?

Today you will tackle your books. Gather any you know you won't read ever again and wouldn't even want to pass on to a friend. These are also perfect to sell on Amazon. If you don't want to list them, then go ahead and donate them to your local library.

Cheers!
Corie
xox

PS. When you're done with this challenge, post a picture on instagram tagging me @corieclark and using the hashtag #simplicityproject

Day 20

Let's Make a Deal!

Have you been collecting items to sell? Today's the day! Gather the items you've set aside and get to work!

You'll need a notepad to write down what each item is selling for and a digital camera or smartphone to snap some pictures. All of the sites offer easy-to-follow guidelines. Don't fret too much over the price; look at what similar items are selling and shipping for and list accordingly.

If you don't have any items set aside to sell then maybe today you need to find some. What can you sell to pay a bill or build your emergency fund?

If you really aren't going to sell anything, then go ahead and spend fifteen minutes tackling the project of your choice.

Cheers!
Corie
xox

PS. When you're done with this challenge, post a picture on instagram tagging me @corieclark and using the hashtag #simplicityproject

Day 21

Last Call

We're in the home stretch. Today I want you to look over your assessment and master list that you made on Day 1.

Are you moving closer to your goal? Do you need to refocus for the week? Make sure that you finish well. If you're disappointed in yourself, don't be! You're doing something and that's all that matters. You have one more week to make this a success.

Decide what you need to do this week so that you are satisfied then make a plan to get it done!

That's it. I want you to rest and plan. Nothing else.

Cheers!
Corie
xox

PS. When you're done with this challenge, post a picture on instagram tagging me @corieclark and using the hashtag #simplicityproject

Day 22

Big Budget

Today you are going to create your Big Budget. This will have every expense you can possibly think of and needs to have a zero balance at the end.

Cheers!
Corie
xox

PS. When you're done with this challenge, post a picture on instagram tagging me @corieclark and using the hashtag #simplicityproject

Day 23

What's In That Closet?

Today you're going to tackle your linen closets and any other closets in your home. Grab your donation box and fill it up. Toss out old sheets and towels that you would be embarrassed to have anyone see. Coats that don't fit your kids because they've grown six inches since the last time they wore them--in the box they go.

Chances are you'll find items that have been shoved or hidden in your closets that don't belong there. Find them a home or get rid of them.

Cheers!
Corie
xox

PS. When you're done with this challenge, post a picture on instagram tagging me @corieclark and using the hashtag #simplicityproject

Day 24

Your Choice

Spend thirty minutes today working on that dreaded project that you've been putting off for far too long.

That garage that is bursting at the seams. The photo bin that hasn't been sorted. The taxes you still haven't filed. The doctor's appointment you need to make. The phone call that you've been dreading.

There are so many things we put off because we're afraid to face them. Today is the day. I promise, when you face your fear it will look so much easier to defeat.

Cheers!
Corie
xox

PS. When you're done with this challenge, post a picture on instagram tagging me @corieclark and using the hashtag #simplicityproject

Day 25

Laundry Time

Today you are going to de-clutter the laundry area of your home. Clean laundry still lingering? Put it away. Single socks that still haven't found their match? Toss 'em or add them to your cleaning rag collection. Empty bottles and half-used products you'll never finish?

Gone.

Completely clear off the top of the washer and dryer and wipe it down so it's sparkly!

Cheers!
Corie
xox

PS. When you're done with this challenge, post a picture on instagram tagging me @corieclark and using the hashtag #simplicityproject

Day 26

Debt be Gone

If you're trying to get out of debt and still have credit cards at your disposal, you're climbing a slippery slope. If you've been able to set aside $1,000 in an emergency fund, then today, I want you to make an extra payment on a debt or pay one off completely!

The freedom that comes from a life without credit card debt is indescribable. If you don't have the emergency fund, then I want you to come up with a plan to get it as quickly as possible. What can you sell? Can you babysit for a friend? Take care of a pet? Mow some lawns? There has got to be something you can do! Think about what you're good at and what others need and offer your services!

Cheers!
Corie
xox

PS. When you're done with this challenge, post a picture on instagram tagging me @corieclark and using the hashtag #simplicityproject

Day 27

Drop it Like it's Hot

{Because who says you can't dance and organize at the same time?}

Today you're going to drop off all of the donations you've been gathering over the last few weeks. Hopefully they're already in your trunk and ready to go. You can donate to a local women's shelter, thrift store, or even the Salvation Army. Wherever you decide, just get it done today!

Cheers!
Corie
xox

PS. When you're done with this challenge, post a picture on instagram tagging me @corieclark and using the hashtag #simplicityproject

Day 28

You Won!

Congratulations! You survived the 28-Day Simplicity Project! I'm so proud of you!

Whether you did every task or you only did five, you did something. Today I want you to rest and reflect on how far you've come. If you feel like you've barely made a dent, then go ahead and jump in again.

Maybe you've made headway and now you need to just focus on one specific area of your life. Go back and read through that particular section of the book and make a commitment to tackle that area once and for all.

Decide what you're going to do this next week to move towards a life of simplicity and start living a life of purpose. Write it down and do it. The world is waiting for you!

Cheers!
Corie
xox

PS. When you're done with this challenge, post a picture on instagram tagging me @corieclark and using the hashtag #simplicityproject

Notes

1. SOAP, http://soapstudy.com/
2. Steven Covey, First Things First, {Free Press; Reprint edition, 1996}

About the Author

Corie Clark is passionate about helping people find their purpose and truly live it to its fullest. Corie is married to her best friend, Ryan and has three beautiful children.

Since originally writing The Simplicity Project in 2014, she has grown to become a personal brand expert, creator of The Purposeful Planner, and podcast host of "Purpose with Corie Clark."

She is passionate about helping women discover their God-given purpose and turn it into a life and business they love. She helps purpose-driven women uplevel their personal brand to a six and seven figure business through her Purpose Babe Society and Purposeful Influence Mastermind.

Keep up with Corie and check out her programs to dive deeper into walking out your purpose at

CorieClark.com
Instagram.com/corieclark
Facebook.com/corieclarkpurpose
#TheSimplicityProject

Made in the USA
Middletown, DE
21 July 2022